A GUIDE TO

A CLOCKWORK ORANGE

SEAN SHEEHAN

WITH TONY BUZAN

Hodder & Stoughton

ISBN 0 340 80305 3

First published 2001
Impression number   10 9 8 7 6 5 4 3 2 1
Year   2006 2005 2004 2003 2002 2001

Cover photograph: Donald Cooper, Photostage
Mind Maps: Kate Boyd

Typeset by Transet Limited, Coventry, England.
Printed in Great Britain for Hodder & Stoughton Educational, a division of
Hodder Headline Plc, 338 Euston Road, London NW1 3BH by Cox and Wyman Ltd,
Reading, Berks.

CONTENTS

REVISION FOR A-LEVEL LITERATURE SUCCESS

You are now in the most important educational stage of your life, and are soon to take English Literature exams that may have a major impact on your future career and goals. As one A-level student put it: 'It's crunch time!'

At this crucial stage of your life the one thing you need even more than subject knowledge is the knowledge of *how* to remember, *how* to read faster, *how* to comprehend, *how* to study, *how* to take notes and *how* to organize your thoughts. You need to know how to *think*; you need a basic introduction on how to use that super bio-computer inside your head – your brain.

The next eight pages contain a goldmine of information on how you can achieve success both at school and in your A-level English Literature exams, as well as in your professional or university career. These eight pages will give you skills that will enable you to be successful in *all* your academic pursuits. You will learn:

◆ How to recall more *while* you are learning.
◆ How to recall more *after* you have finished a class or a study period.
◆ How to use special techniques to improve your memory.
◆ How to use a revolutionary note-taking technique called Mind Maps that will double your memory and help you to write essays and answer exam questions.
◆ How to read everything faster while at the same time improving your comprehension and concentration.
◆ How to zap your revision!

How to understand, improve and master your memory of Literature Guides

Your memory really is like a muscle. Don't exercise it and it will grow weaker; *do* exercise it properly and it will grow incredibly more powerful. There are really only four main things you need to understand about your memory in order to increase its power dramatically:

Recall during learning
– YOU MUST TAKE BREAKS!

When you are studying, your memory can concentrate, understand and recall well for between 20 and 45 minutes at a time. Then it *needs* a break. If you carry on for longer than this without one, your memory starts to break down. If you study for hours non-stop, you will remember only a fraction of what you have been trying to learn, and you will have wasted valuable revision time.

So, ideally, *study for less than an hour,* then take a five- to ten-minute break. During this break listen to music, go for a walk, do some exercise, or just daydream. (Daydreaming is a necessary brain-power booster – geniuses do it regularly.) During the break your brain will be sorting out what it has been learning and you will go back to your study with the new information safely stored and organized in your memory banks. Make *sure* you take breaks at regular intervals as you work through the *Literature Guides.*

Recall after learning
– SURFING THE WAVES OF YOUR MEMORY

What do you think begins to happen to your memory straight *after* you have finished learning something? Does it immediately start forgetting? No! Surprisingly, your brain actually *increases* its power and carries on remembering. For a short time after your study session, your brain integrates the information, making a more complete picture of everything it has just learnt. Only then does the rapid decline in memory begin, as much as 80 per cent of what you have learnt can be forgotten in a day.

However, if you catch the top of the wave of your memory, and briefly review what you have been revising at the correct time, the memory is stamped in far more strongly, and stays at the crest of the wave for a much longer time. To maximize your brain's power to remember, take a few minutes and use a Mind Map to review what you have learnt at the end of a day. Then review it at the end of a week, again at the end of a month, and finally a week before the exams. That way you'll surf-ride your memory wave all the way to your exam, success and beyond!

The memory principle of association

The muscle of your memory becomes stronger when it can **associate** – when it can link things together.

Think about your best friend, and all the things your mind *automatically* links with that person. Think about your favourite hobby, and all the associations your mind has when you think about (remember!) that hobby.

When you are studying, use this memory principle to make associations between the elements in your subjects, and thus to improve both your memory and your chances of success.

The memory principle of imagination

The muscle of your memory will improve significantly if you can produce big images in your mind. Rather than just memorizing the name of a character, imagine that character of the novel or play as if you were a video producer filming that person's life. The same goes for images in poetry.

In *all* your subjects use the **imagination** memory principle.

Throughout this *Literature Guide* you will find special association and imagination techniques (called mnemonics after the Greek goddess Mnemosyne) that will make it much easier for you to remember the topic being discussed. Look out for them!

Your new success formula: Mind Maps®

You have noticed that when people go on holidays, or travel, they take maps. Why? To give them a general picture of where they are going, to help them locate places of special interest and importance, to help them find things more easily, and to help them remember distances and locations, etc.

It is exactly the same with your mind and with study. If you have a 'map of the territory' of what you have to learn, then everything is easier. In learning and study, the Mind Map is that special tool.

As well as helping you with all areas of study, the Mind Map actually *mirrors the way your brain works.* Your Mind Maps can be used for taking notes from your study books, for taking notes in class, for preparing your homework, for presenting your homework, for reviewing your tests, for checking your and your friends' knowledge in any subject, and for *helping you understand anything you learn.* Mind Maps are especially useful in English literature, as they allow you to map out the whole territory of a novel, play or poem, giving you an 'at-a-glance' snapshot of all the key information you need to know.

The Mind Maps in the *Literature Guide* use, throughout, **imagination** and **association**. As such, they automatically strengthen your memory muscle every time you use them. Throughout this guide you will find Mind Maps that summarize the most important areas of the English Literature guide you are studying. Study these Mind Maps, add some colour, personalize them, and then have a go at making your own Mind Maps of the work you are studying – you will remember them far better! Put them on your walls and in your files for a quick and easy review. Mind Maps are fast, efficient, effective and, importantly, *fun* to do!

HOW TO DRAW A MIND MAP

1 Start in the middle of the page with the page turned sideways. This gives your brain more radiant freedom for its thoughts.

2 Always start by drawing a picture or symbol of the novel or its title. Why? Because *a picture is worth a thousand words to your brain.* Try to use at least three colours, as colour helps your memory even more.

3 Let your thoughts flow, and write or draw your ideas on coloured branching lines connected to your central image. The key symbols and words are the headings for your topic.

4 Next, add facts and ideas by drawing more, smaller, branches on to the appropriate main branches, just like a tree.

5 Always print your word clearly on its line. Use only one word per line.

6 To link ideas and thoughts on different branches, use arrows, colours, underlining and boxes.

HOW TO READ A MIND MAP

1 Begin in the centre, the focus of your novel, play or poem.

2 The words/images attached to the centre are like chapter headings; read them next.

3 Always read out from the centre, in every direction (even on the left-hand side, where you will read from right to left, instead of the usual left to right).

USING MIND MAPS

Mind Maps are a versatile tool – use them for taking notes in class or from books, for solving problems, for brainstorming with friends, and for reviewing and revising for exams – their uses are infinite! You will find them invaluable for planning essays for coursework and exams. Number your main branches in the order in which you want to use them and off you go – the main headings for your essay are done and all your ideas are logically organized!

*S*uper speed reading and study

What do you think happens to your comprehension as your reading speed rises? 'It goes down!' Wrong! It seems incredible, but it has been proved – the faster you read, the more you comprehend and remember!

So here are some tips to help you to practise reading faster – you'll cover the ground much more quickly, remember more, *and* have more time for revision and leisure activities!

SUPER SPEED READING

1 First read the whole text (whether it's a lengthy book or an exam paper) very quickly, to give your brain an overall idea of what's ahead and get it working. (It's like sending out a scout to look at the territory you have to cover – it's much easier when you know what to expect!) Then read the text again for more detailed information.
2 Have the text a reasonable distance away from your eyes. In this way your eye/brain system will be able to see more at a glance, and will naturally begin to read faster.
3 Take in groups of words at a time. Rather than reading 'slowly and carefully' read faster, more enthusiastically. Your comprehension will rocket!
4 Take in phrases rather than single words while you read.
5 Use a guide. Your eyes are designed to follow movement, so a thin pencil underneath the lines you are reading, moved smoothly along, will 'pull' your eyes to faster speeds.

HOW TO MAKE STUDY EASY FOR YOUR BRAIN

When you are going somewhere, is it easier to know beforehand where you are going, or not? Obviously it is easier if you *do* know. It is the same for your brain and a book. When you get a new book, there are seven things you can do to help your brain get to 'know the territory' faster:

1 Scan through the whole book in less than 20 minutes, as you would do if you were in a shop thinking whether or not to buy it. This gives your brain *control*.

2 Think about what you already know about the subject.
   You'll often find out it's a lot more than you thought. A good
   way of doing this is to do a quick Mind Map on *everything
   you know* after you have skimmed through it.

3 Ask who, what, why, where, when and how questions about
   what is in the book. Questions help your brain 'fish' the
   knowledge out.

4 Ask your friends what they know about the subject. This
   helps them review the knowledge in their own brains, and
   helps your brain get new knowledge about what you are
   studying.

5 Have another quick speed read through the book, this time
   looking for any diagrams, pictures and illustrations, and also
   at the beginnings and ends of chapters. Most information is
   contained in the beginnings and ends.

6 If you come across any difficult parts in your book, mark
   them and *move on*. Your brain *will* be able to solve the
   problems when you come back to them a bit later. Much
   like saving the difficult bits of a jigsaw puzzle for later.
   When you have finished the book, quickly review it one
   more time and then discuss it with friends. This will lodge it
   permanently in your memory banks.

7 Build up a Mind Map as you study the book. This helps
   your brain to organize and hold (remember!) information as
   you study.

Helpful hints for exam revision

◆ To avoid **exam panic** cram at the *start* of your course, not
  the end. It takes the same amount of time, so you may as
  well use it where it is best placed!

◆ Use Mind Maps throughout your course, and build a Master
  Mind Map for each subject – a giant Mind Map that
  summarizes everything you know about the subject.

◆ Use memory techniques such as mnemonics (verses or
  systems for remembering things like dates and events or
  lists).

◆ Get together with one or two friends to revise, compare
  Mind Maps, and discuss topics.

AND FINALLY ...

◆ *Have fun while you learn* – studies show that those people who enjoy what they are doing understand and remember it more, and generally do better.

◆ *Use your teachers* as resource centres. Ask them for help with specific topics and with more general advice on how you can improve your all-round performance.

◆ *Personalize your* **Literature Revision Guide** by underlining and highlighting, by adding notes and pictures. Allow your brain to have a conversation with it!

Your *amazing brain and its amazing cells*

Your brain is like a super, *super, SUPER* computer. The world's best computers have only a few thousand or hundred thousand computer chips. Your brain has 'computer chips' too, and they are called brain cells. Unlike the computer, you do not have only a few thousand computer chips – the number of brain cells in your head is a *million MILLION*!! This means you are a genius just waiting to discover yourself! All you have to do is learn how to get those brain cells working together, and you'll not only become more smart, you'll have more free time to pursue your other fun activities.

The more you understand your amazing brain the more it will repay and amaze you!

Apply its power to this *Literature Guide*!

(Tony Buzan)

HOW TO USE THIS GUIDE

This guide assumes that you have already read *A Clockwork Orange*, although you could read 'Context' and 'The story of *A Clockwork Orange*' first. It is best to use the guide alongside the novel. You could read the 'Characterization' and 'Themes' sections without referring to the novel, but you will get more out of these if you do.

The sections

The 'Commentary' section can be used in a number of ways. One way is to read a chapter of the novel, and then read the relevant commentary. Keep on until you come to a test section, test yourself – then have a break! Alternatively, read the Commentary for a chapter, then read that chapter in the novel, then go back to the Commentary. See what works best for you.

'Critical approaches' sums up the main critical views and interpretations of the novel. Your own response is important, but be aware of these approaches too.

'How to get an "A" in English Literature' gives valuable advice on what to look for in a text, and what skills you need to develop in order to achieve your personal best.

'The exam essay' is a useful 'night before' reminder of how to tackle exam questions, though it will help you more if you also look at it much earlier in the year. 'Model answer and essay plan' gives an example A-grade essay and the Mind Map and plan used to write it.

The questions

Whenever you come across a question in the guide with a star ✪ in front of it, think about it for a moment. You could make a Mini Mind Map or a few notes to focus your mind. There is not usually a 'right' answer to these: it is important for you to develop your own opinions if you want to get an 'A'. The 'Test' sections are designed to take you about 15–20 minutes each – time well spent. Take a short break after each one.

Key to icons

A **theme** is an idea explored by an author. Whenever a theme is dealt with in the guide, the appropriate icon is used. This means you can find where a theme is mentioned just by flicking through the book. Go on – try it now!

Free will		Dystopia	
Violence		Crime and punishment	
Youth culture		Growing up	

LANGUAGE, STYLE AND STRUCTURE

This heading and icon are used in the Commentary wherever there is a special section on the author's choice of words and imagery, and the overall plot structure.

Anthony Burgess' life

Anthony Burgess was born in 1917 in England and educated at Manchester University. After serving as a soldier during World War II, Burgess took up a post as an education officer in Malaya (now the independent republic of Malaysia but at the time a part of the British Empire). In 1959 he returned to Britain, having being diagnosed as suffering from a terminal illness, and devoted himself full-time to writing in the hope that he could provide his wife with some financial security after his death. The diagnosis proved mistaken but Burgess never gave up his new career and he ended up writing more than thirty novels and other books.

In 1962, the year after the Russians launched the first man into space, *A Clockwork Orange*, his eighth novel, was published. Links between the story and his own life are related by Burgess in his autobiography, *You've Had Your Time*. His first wife had been viciously attacked in London during World War II by a group of four deserters from the US army. When he and his wife returned to England from Malaya, they witnessed street fights between rival youth gangs, known as Mods and Rockers at the time. Burgess saw how the energy of youth could express itself in street gangs and fights and the idea for a story began to take shape.

The film and the book

The first attempt to film the book, in the middle of the 1960s, was to feature the rock group The Rolling Stones and Mick Jagger in the role of Alex. Burgess approved of the choice of actor, calling Jagger the 'quintessence of delinquency'. This never came to anything and it was left to Stanley Kubrick, a noted director, to make a film of the novel. However, he based his version of *A Clockwork Orange* on American editions of the text. When the book had first appeared in an American edition, the last chapter was missing completely and the story ended with the final ironic words of Chapter 6, *I was cured all right*. This culling of the last chapter was deliberate because the American publisher thought it would make a better ending for the book. 'The tough tradition of American popular fiction ousted what was termed British blandness,' explained Burgess in his autobiography. He confesses that he knew about the final chapter being lopped off at the time but agreed to it because he needed the cash advance offered by the publisher.

Nowadays, American editions of the book do carry the final chapter. However, a permanent legacy of its earlier omission is that Kubrick followed the American edition when he came to film the book. It seems that the film director was unaware of the missing chapter and that Burgess himself was unaware of how the film would end until he saw it for the first time.

The film received a lot of attention after its release and it was not long before a violent crime was linked to the film. It was reported that four boys, dressed in a style resembling the *droogs* of the film, had raped a nun in New York State after watching the film. It turned out that while a rape had been committed, the boys had not seen the film. The film was withdrawn from circulation in Britain by Kubrick and only recently, after the death of the film director, has it once again become publicly available in Britain. Kubrick's reputation as a highly regarded director is closely associated with his film of *A Clockwork Orange*, as well as his science-fiction film *2001*.

Part 1

A Clockwork Orange, written in 1962, is set about a decade into the future. The story begins in a milk bar where drinks are ordered with a choice of **drugs**. Alex, the narrator, introduces himself to the reader and explains how he is the leader of a gang of four delinquent youths. Their **criminal** activities include attacking people, usually with a view to robbing them, and committing rape when an opportunity arises. They live in a **violent society** where crime is increasing and where social groups are very isolated from each other. **Youth gangs** are common, elderly poor people are seen huddling in pubs for company and better-off households stay indoors at night watching satellite television broadcasts.

Alex has a passion for classical music, especially Beethoven, and **Dim**, one of his gang, ridicules a woman in a pub for singing from an opera that Alex enjoys. Alex hits Dim for his bad manners and this exposes tensions within the gang over Alex's leadership. After violently attacking Dim in the street, **Georgie**, another member of the gang, is also challenged by Alex to a fight. The fourth member of the gang, **Pete**, declines the challenge and avoids fighting. Behind Alex's back, the gang members conspire to set up their leader during the course of another violent robbery. The woman whose house Alex had burgled dies later as a result of injuries received in the break-in and the police are waiting to arrest Alex. Part 1 draws to an end in a police station where Alex is now on the receiving end of some violence and can expect a long prison sentence. He is 15 years of age.

Part 2

The seven chapters of Part 2 all take place in a prison and a special unit where Alex is subjected to a course of treatment called **Ludovico's Technique**. This method of treating violent criminals has been introduced by an authoritarian government keen to win a forthcoming election by being seen to have reduced the crime rate. Alex is selected for the treatment after an incident in his overcrowded cell leads to one of the prisoners being beaten to death. Ludovico's Technique is a form of **conditioning** designed to form an association in the mind between violence and physical pain so that whenever Alex sees or thinks of something involving violence he experiences physical reactions that drive him to behave in a passive, socially acceptable manner. Alex will no longer have a choice in the matter: he will be conditioned to act in the way he does.

The prison **chaplain** raises **ethical objections** to this form of treatment. He argues that the exercise of **free will** is fundamental to being human and if this is taken away then a person is reduced to the level of a machine, an automaton. This links in with the title of a book that was being written by the man whose house was broken into by Alex in Part 1. The title, *A Clockwork Orange*, is an image that captures the sense of something natural being forced to behave like a mechanism. The chaplain's objections are brushed aside by the government and the doctor in charge, who only see the need to reduce the crime rate and the prison population. The government is not motivated by humanitarian feelings; it wants to fill the prisons with a growing number of political prisoners.

Alex is 'cured' of his violent tendencies and released early from prison after just two years. Proof that he has been cured comes in the form of a demonstration that has Alex trying to lick the boots of an assailant in a desperate attempt to avoid further violence.

Part 3

Alex leaves prison in a blaze of **publicity** as living proof of the government's success in tackling crime. He returns to his parents' home only to discover a lodger using his bedroom and his music collection confiscated by the government. Alex would like to assault the lodger but knows he cannot afford to feel aggressive because this will make him start to feel physically sick.

Worse is to come when Alex visits a music store to listen to some of his favourite music. He discovers that the conditioning is a crude technique and, because Beethoven's music provided a soundtrack during the course of his treatment, he also experiences physical pain whenever he hears something like it. Alex is driven to **despair** and visits a library to find information on suicide. Here he is violently attacked by a former victim of his and Alex has to be rescued by the police. One of the policemen who drives him away for a beating is none other than Dim.

Alex happens to be rescued by **F. Alexander**, the man whose wife Alex raped two years earlier. F. Alexander is also the man who was writing a book called *A Clockwork Orange*. Not recognized at first, Alex becomes a pawn in a **political** struggle between the government and an opposition seeking to bring it down. Opponents of the government lock Alex in a room where he can hear music played incessantly, driving him to attempt suicide by throwing himself out of the window. The plan backfires and Alex is restored to his normal state of mind in a hospital, with the government taking credit once again.

Alex meets his previous fellow gang member Pete, and is surprised to discover he has married and settled down to a peaceful way of life. Alex realizes that he too is **changing** and, although he has formed a new teenage gang, violence no longer has the same attraction for him. He now seeks a girlfriend with whom he can settle down, though he is aware that a son of his own might have to go through the difficult period of **growing up** that he has experienced himself.

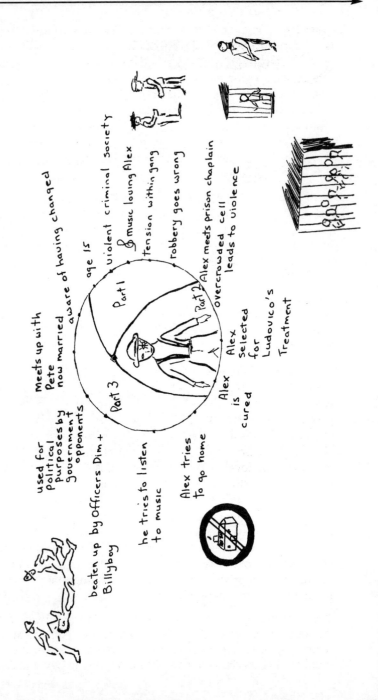

age 15
violent criminal society
music loving Alex
tension within gang
robbery goes wrong

Part 1

Part 2

Alex meets prison chaplain
Overcrowded cell leads to violence

Alex selected for Ludovico's Treatment

Alex is cured

Alex tries to go home

he tries to listen to music

Part 3

beaten up by Officers Dim + Billyboy

used for political purposes by government opponents

Meets up with Pete now married

aware of having changed

CHARACTERIZATION

The Mini Mind Map above summarizes the main characters in *A Clockwork Orange*. When you have read this section, look at the full Mind Map on p. 13, then make a copy of the Mini Mind Map and try to add to it from memory.

In one sense, there is only one character in the story and that is Alex himself. Burgess is not interested in peopling his novel with a rich array of characters, all with their own complex psychologies, and chooses instead to focus on one main character. This is an aspect of his **characterization** (the way characters are presented) and the other characters are necessarily undeveloped by comparison. *A Clockwork Orange* is very much a story with a central idea and Alex is the character who embodies this idea. The other characters feed into this central idea and contribute by way of the positions and attitudes they take up and the roles they play in Alex's development, but they are not characters of intrinsic interest. A good example of this type of characterization is found in the portrayal of the prison chaplain: his role is important, but he is not developed in any psychological depth as a character.

✪ Compare the characterization of *A Clockwork Orange* with that of other works of literature you are studying. If you are reading Shakespeare, Dickens or Jane Austen consider the number of characters with an individual psychology that they introduce compared with Burgess. Are you reading any text that also focuses on just one main character?

Alex

Alex's individual personality is expressed through his use of language and the very particular high regard he has for standards of personal appearance and cleanliness. In Chapter 1, he seems to take some pride in describing the dress code for his youth culture and he tidies up Dim after the attack on the shopkeepers. He rails against the drunk in Chapter 2 for not caring about his appearance and remarks on the body odour of Billyboy, a rival gang leader. There are plenty of other examples to be found throughout the book and as you read you should underline or mark those places where Alex comments on body language and body hygiene. Alex's sensitivity to personal appearance may be seen partly as an aspect of his youth and partly as an expression of his sense of *dignity*. He is only 15 at the start of the story and despite his callous violence there is a certain naive innocence about him that reflects his age. The account of his experiences in prison, before he is selected for treatment, confirms this impression of his youthful innocence.

The most distinctive assertion of Alex's individuality is his love of classical music, because this sets him apart from his friends and his age group. The attack on his individuality as a result of Ludovico's Technique is symbolized by the way he becomes unable to enjoy his favourite music. It is difficult not to feel sorry for Alex after his release from prison and his naivety is again revealed when he becomes a pawn in a political struggle between the government and an opposition party.

A unique aspect of Alex's characterization is that the reader sees how he undergoes change and development. Other characters change in some respects but their basic outlook on life and their inner self do not alter. Two examples of this would be Dim and Billyboy becoming policemen. Pete does undergo a change in character similar to Alex, for he also grows up and senses his new state of adulthood, but the reader is not invited to share this development. It is just presented as a fact. With Alex, on the other hand, the reader gets to know him and follows his changing fortunes and his gradual realization that he is changing.

Dim and Pete

There is another gang member, Georgie, but he dies while Alex is in prison. The characterization of Dim and Pete is more important because, as they are just a little older than Alex himself, we also see them growing up over a period of two to three years. Dim develops but does not really change; he merely exchanges his gang outfit for a police uniform. Pete does change and mature but the reader does not share his experiences.

In their youth, the characterization of Dim and Pete complements that of Alex and shows the callous violence of their society. Alex is not evil in the sense of being possessed by a unique individual need to hurt and cause pain to others. Dim and Pete, and Georgie for that matter, behave in a similar way and this suggests that they are all representatives of their subculture. It is Dim who shows the nastiest nature, the least ability to mature and learn from his experiences, because he is still enjoying violence as an adult whereas Pete and Alex outgrow this as a stage in their growing up.

Chaplain

The chaplain is a very important character in the novel, though more for what he represents than for his individual personality. His ethical objection to Alex's course of treatment is articulated in Chapter 3 of Part 2, although the author underplays his significance by making him an ineffectual and weak man. He knows why the government's new penal policy should be criticized but he fails to live up to his convictions because he is weak-minded and more concerned with holding on to his job. His weak resolve finds refuge in alcohol. We learn in Chapter 6 of Part 3 that he has visited Alex in hospital and told him that he had left the prison service because he couldn't agree with what was happening.

What lends importance to the chaplain is the centrality of his ethics to the moral force of the novel. In an important sense, the chaplain is the voice of the author and many readers come to sense this affinity between what the chaplain says and what the author thinks. Pay careful attention to what the chaplain says and work towards expressing his objections to Alex's treatment in your own words. Memorize at least one quotation where he expresses what is ethically wrong with the government's approach to crime and punishment.

Dr Brodsky

Like the chaplain, Dr Brodsky is more significant for the point of view he expresses than for his individual character. He is responsible for the radical course of treatment that conditions Alex to reject violence and the expression of his philosophy that justifies this treatment is to be found in the last chapter of Part 2. There, before an audience invited to witness the effectiveness of the treatment, Dr Brodsky explains that the sole objective is to reduce the crime rate. He is deaf to the ethical objections raised by the chaplain because, from his point of view, the ethics of the situation are irrelevant. It is a narrow-minded and functional attitude and betrays the limitations of a science that only concerns itself with its own definition of success. As if to emphasize the limitations of this science, the author has Brodsky himself show no interest in music whatsoever.

F. Alexander

F. Alexander plays an important role in the story. When his home is broken into by Alex and his gang, he is writing a book with the title of *A Clockwork Orange*. This naturally alerts the reader and draws attention to the meaning behind the image which gives rise to the title of Burgess' book. In Part 3 of the book, Alex makes an unexpected return visit to his home and by doing so finds himself being used by the government's opponents for a political purpose. F. Alexander's principled objections to the government policy are as valid as those of the chaplain, but in Chapter 5 of Part 3 he is shown to be a little mentally unhinged. The way he sticks a kitchen fork into the wall betrays a violence in his own mind and, as Alex observes, *he was going off his gulliver* [head]. The irony is that his loss of sanity may have something to do with the loss of his wife, a consequence it seems of her brutal beating and rape at the hands of Alex and his gang.

Minor characters

There are a number of minor characters in the story, like Georgie, who has already been mentioned as a member of Alex's gang. More important is the prison governor, who in Chapter 3 of Part 2 expresses an attitude towards crime and punishment that contributes to the novel's concern with this issue. The government minister, the Minister of the Inferior as Burgess delights in being able to call him, is also a minor character who contributes to this debate. He represents the political force that can make use of narrow-minded scientists like Brodsky who do not question the ethical basis of their work. P. R. Deltoid is a minor character, whose attitude towards his work, and Alex in particular, contributes to the theme of crime and punishment and the theme of violence. Billyboy is another minor character, a gang member who like Dim finds an outlet for his violent nature in the police force.

Other minor characters include Alex's parents, well-meaning but ineffectual characters, and a shadowy group of F. Alexander's associates who want to use Alex to discredit the government. These men, D. B. da Silva, Rubinstein and Z. Dolin, are prepared to use Alex in a manner that is not too different from the way the government minister wants to use him. They may be on different political sides, but their disregard for Alex as a person makes them more alike than they would wish to acknowledge.

Over to you

? Take a blank sheet of paper and draw a set of icons for Alex, perhaps using items you associate with him. You may prefer to make your own drawings of them, instead of using icons. Spread them across the page and label them with key words to describe them or scenes that reveal Alex's character and development. Perhaps add quotations from the text that describe Alex at different key moments in the story.

Now that you're clued up on the characters, take a break before considering the themes.

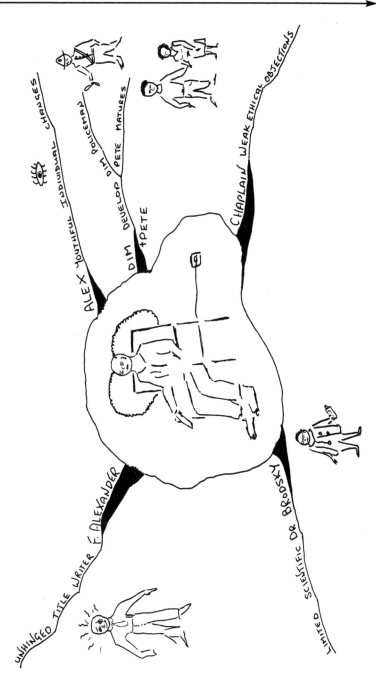

13

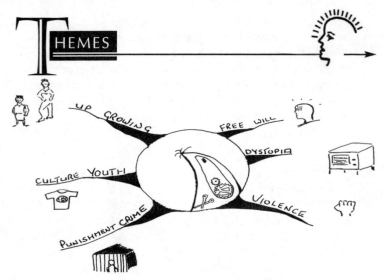

THEMES

A theme is an idea that runs through a work and that is explored and developed along the way. The Mini Mind Map above shows the main themes of *A Clockwork Orange*. Test yourself by copying it and then trying to add to it before comparing your results with the version on p. 21.

The themes of this novel are very closely related and they overlap in a number of ways. When you are reading and studying the book you need to be very aware of this because if you think of them in isolation their depth and significance will be diminished. The theme of violence, for example, relates to all the other themes in varying ways. Violence is viewed as an aspect of the dystopian society of the novel, and it receives its most overt and dramatic expression in the vicious behaviour of street gangs that are part of a youth culture. This results in crimes of various kinds, and the issue of crime and punishment comes into play as the government takes a firm hand in trying to reduce the crime statistics. Alex is a character who is shaped and influenced by this context of violence and who freely and wilfully chooses violence as a way of expressing his own immature nature. In the course of growing up, however, he finds violence to be less satisfying than before and this, combined with an awareness of other needs, like the wish to have a girlfriend, causes him to change and abandon violent behaviour.

Looked at from another point of view, the issue of free will can be seen as the philosophical heart of the novel, with the theme of violence serving to illustrate this. The author, championing the principle of free will as a concept essential to our nature as human beings, proceeds to test this principle by taking violent behaviour as an example. The novel comes to the conclusion that free will is of such fundamental importance that if violent behaviour could be eliminated only by sacrificing free will then this would be too high a price to pay.

Free will

The central importance of this theme is reflected in the author's choice of title for his book. Its significance is explained in Chapter 2 when Alex reads from the manuscript in the cottage and discovers that the man is writing a book with the same title. The man is arguing that because a person is a living, developing being, a *creature of growth and capable of sweetness* (like an orange), it is not right to impose on people mechanical laws that treat them like bits of machinery – hence a clockwork orange. The next key moment comes in Chapter 4 when Alex thinks about goodness and badness and the importance of making a choice. In Chapter 3 of Part 2 the chaplain applies such an ethic to the government's new plan to deal with violent individuals.

The theme of free will is at the heart of the novel and Burgess poses a dilemma concerning the topic. If a scientific method could be developed for conditioning people's attitudes, would it be desirable to employ it? ❍ If scientists developed the means of genetically engineering people's behaviour, would it represent progress? There can be little doubt that Burgess would reply with an emphatic 'no'. The fact that the reader can feel so sure of what the author's opinion is raises another dilemma, namely whether a novel can still be a work of art when the author is presenting a particular point of view. Works of literature that present only one point of view are usually labelled **didactic**. This is usually viewed as a fault, and this criticism has been levelled at *A Clockwork Orange*. To see why such a charge does not really apply to this novel, turn to the 'Critical approaches' section of this guide.

Although it is not mentioned in the novel, the kind of conditioning that Alex undergoes is associated with the work of Pavlov, a Russian physiologist who became famous for his experiments on the conditioning of animals. It is also associated with an American psychologist, B. F. Skinner, whose ideas underpin techniques of 'programmed learning' that seek to reinforce learning by immediate and regular feedback.

Dystopia

A dystopia is an imaginary place or condition in which everything is as bad as possible. It is the opposite of a utopia, an imaginary world where everything is perfect. The dystopia of *A Clockwork Orange* does not consist only of the government's disastrous attempt to brainwash young people so as to get re-elected. This is just the most dramatic case of a society that has many objectionable features, one of which is the high crime rate which motivates the government to adopt a drastic method in the first place.

The novel's dystopia is not set in some futuristic science-fiction world. Burgess himself was projecting the action only about a decade into the future. Like many of the dystopias created by other novelists – Orwell's *1984*, Bradbury's *Fahrenheit 451* or Huxley's *Brave New World*, for example – the creation of an unpleasant, though imaginary, society is built up from aspects of the contemporary world. The novelist then exaggerates these aspects, or follows them through to their logical conclusions, in order to make a moral judgement about the way our own society might be heading. Works of literature that imagine a future society nearly always reveal more about the contemporary society of the author than they do about a possible future alternative.

The dystopian future of *A Clockwork Orange* is not a mere backdrop to the story, as if it is the novel's equivalent to a central piece of stage scenery. Burgess sees Alex as a product of the dystopian society in which he lives, and his antisocial behaviour is one aspect of the horribly dysfunctional community in which he grows up. The same can be said of the three themes of youth culture, violence and of crime and punishment. In their different ways, they all explore and comment on the kind of society that Burgess imagines could emerge from British society. ✪ What aspects, if any, of your present-day society do you see as suggesting the dystopian world of *A Clockwork Orange*?

Violence

The themes of violence and dystopia are closely related in that a culture of violence is one of the defining characteristics of the dystopian society of *A Clockwork Orange*. At the start of the novel the violence is depicted in the context of teenage gangs but it gradually becomes clear that the young teenagers are not acting like this in isolation. The police and the prison authorities also take violence for granted and, in the case of the adoption of Ludovico's Technique, the government is also prepared to endorse violent methods to gain popularity with the voters and stay in power. The violence of Ludovico's Technique is not of the same kind as the violence of Alex and his *droogs* [friends] but it shares with it a willingness to ignore people's rights and impose upon them something harmful. This is summed up visually by the spectacle of Alex being tied into a chair and having his eyelids forced open.

In his autobiography, Burgess refers to the importance of this theme when he comments on the reaction to the film version of his novel: 'As for the terrible theme – the violence of the individual preferable to the violence of the state – questions were asked in parliament and the banning of the film was urged.' The author is here making explicit an idea that emerges in the novel, that violence by the state cannot be justified on the grounds that it is dealing with violent individuals. Moreover, in a test case like the one dramatized in the novel, the individual's rights are more important than the state's rights. The state cannot use a technique that is violent in nature in order to deal with violence, or at least it cannot do so without sinking to the same level as that of the violent anti-social individual. The right to make an ethical choice, even if this means choosing to be violent, is so important that it overrides a government policy that rests on removing that right. This, of course, brings the theme of free will into the equation as well.

Crime and punishment

What is the best way of dealing with crime and what part should punishment play in dealing with the criminal? This is a question to which there are different answers and some of the different possible responses are explored in *A Clockwork Orange*. The prison governor, in Chapter 3 of Part 2, speaks of the need for retribution, *an eye for an eye*, and Burgess does not avoid accepting the persuasiveness of a wish for vengeance. According to the government minister, F. Alexander was informed by his associates that Alex was one of those who broke into his house in the expectation that would drive F. Alexander to seek revenge. The book presents enough graphic descriptions of acts of sexual violence to make the reader understand why someone might feel that retribution should play a part in dealing with criminals.

To the government minister, the solution to crime is simple – *kill the criminal reflex* – and Dr Brodsky is able to provide a means of doing so. This, as we have seen, raises a serious ethical issue about the exercise of free will. This is also an example of the way in which two of the themes – free will and crime and punishment – overlap.

Ways of punishing a criminal ought to take some account of the circumstances relating to the crime. P. R. Deltoid cannot understand how someone like Alex could be so inclined to violence and criminality, but the themes of violence and dystopia help the reader gain a sense of the kind of environment in which Alex grows up. This does not excuse Alex's criminal behaviour but it does make it more understandable. The way prison life is presented in Part 2 contributes to this sociological understanding of crime.

Youth culture

Burgess observed the youth culture of gangs of his own times, the Mods and the Rockers who fought on the beach fronts of seaside towns in the south of England. He saw the phenomenon developing into a major social problem because of the *aimless energy of these new young, well-fed with money in their pockets.* He sees history as providing other examples of its own, and in his autobiography he quotes an example from the 1590s when youths rioted in London. He first had the idea of setting his story in such an historical context but then warmed to the idea of a prophetic story in which a government might feel forced to adopt drastic measures to deal with increasing youth violence.

The author looks at youth culture as a form of identity whereby young people find forms of expression that appeal to them. This explains the emphasis on details of gang dress and the way fashion codes work within a youth culture. The theme of youth culture overlaps with the theme of growing up. At the end of the book, Alex has matured and the gang culture of which he once felt a part is beginning to lose its appeal for him.

Growing up

Burgess' description of his book's structure in his autobiography points to the importance of this theme in the novel: 'It was divided into three sections of seven chapters each, the total figure being, in traditional arithmology, the symbol of human maturity.' Built into the structure was the space for growth and development, and the novel takes the shape of young Alex growing up and renouncing violence as a childish aspect of his youth. The author explains in his autobiography that this – the capacity for change on the part of the central character – is what makes the story a 'genuine if brief novel'.

The American edition of the novel ended with Chapter 6 of Part 3 because, as Burgess put it, the publisher wanted 'Alex to be a figure in a fable, not a novel'. For the author, a novel carries with it the possibility of change and development and, by having Alex remain unchanged by his experiences, the American edition ruled this out.

In his autobiography Burgess notes how when he first observed youth gangs fighting in England, they 'seemed to love aggression for its own sake'. This, as seen in the previous section, relates the themes of violence and youth culture, and both of these themes can be viewed as aspects of growing up.

At the end of the book, with Alex emerging as a mature adult, the appeal of belonging to a gang is fast fading away. Similarly, the Alex of the last chapter is no longer excited at the prospect of violence, something which is represented by him keeping a photograph of a baby in his pocket.

The novel's conclusion presents growing up as part of a natural cycle of life. Alex thinks of his son going through a similar process: *and so it would itty* [go] *on to like the end of the world, round and round and round.*

Over to you again

? Take a sheet of paper and draw the theme icons across it. Think about how they connect and overlap. For example, the kind of youth culture portrayed in the book is part of the broader dystopian view of society. Draw lines to link the themes and label them with keywords to show the connections.

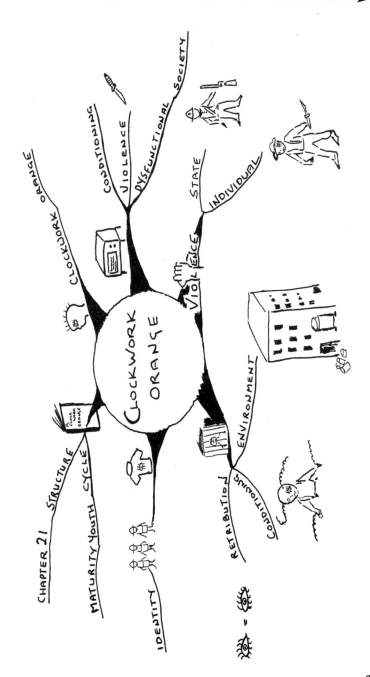

L ANGUAGE, STYLE AND STRUCTURE

Language

Burgess, after first conceiving the story that became the plot of *A Clockwork Orange*, put his draft version away in a drawer because, he said, he faced a problem that was 'wholly stylistic'. He knew that the story would have to be told by a youth and he knew that if he adopted contemporary slang of the 1960s this would inevitably become outdated. It took a holiday in Russia, for which he started relearning the language, for the idea to come to him that he could use Russian to solve his stylistic problem. The Russian suffix for -teen was *nasdat* and this became his name for the teenage dialect.

Part of the pleasure in reading *A Clockwork Orange* consists of translating the words and understanding what is being said. Help is provided in this guide, but in the course of reading the book you should compile your own dictionary by guessing and working out the meaning of the words used. Burgess has used the Russian language to supply many of the words, adapting them where he sees fit. 'Khorosho', for example, is Russian for 'good' or 'well' and this becomes *horrorshow*; 'iudi', meaning 'people', becomes *lewdies* and 'militsia' (the police) becomes *millicents*. Burgess also uses a smattering of rhyming slang so that *pretty polly* (rhyming with lolly) stands for money. Sometimes the author just enjoys making up words like *appy polly loggy* (apology) and *skolliwoll* (school), or using a shortened form like *pee and em* (pop and mom) or *sinny* (cinema).

Burgess also had an **aesthetic** purpose in introducing *nasdat*. He knew his novel would deal with extreme violence and hoped that his use of language would act as 'a kind of mist half-hiding the mayhem and protecting the reader from his own baser instincts' (extract from Burgess' autobiography). The *nasdat* would act as a linguistic fog, preventing the reader from being uncomfortably close to realistic descriptions of violence.

Set against this street **argot** is the distinctive personal voice of Alex himself. He likes to speak in a slightly old-fashioned manner, using characteristic phrases like *O my brothers*, and this sets him apart from the rest of his gang. His use of language becomes a part of his personality, lending him a personable character that helps endear him to the reader.

*S*tyle

A Clockwork Orange is a short novel and invites the compressed style of writing that Burgess brings to it. The author chooses not to write long descriptive passages, even though other novels of his show he is quite capable of this, or to digress or use a subplot. The writing style has a very visual quality and it is therefore not surprising that a film version was made. Do not make the mistake, however, of confusing the style of the novel with the style of Kubrick's film. Take, for example, the description of the encounter between the rival gangs of Alex and Billyboy in Chapter 2. It is not difficult to visualize this scene played out on a cinema screen because of the compact and highly visual way in which Burgess describes what is happening. Two examples would be: *she ran with her thin white legs flashing through the dark, still going 'Oh oh oh.'* and *it was real satisfaction to me to waltz – left two three, right two three – and carve left cheeky and right cheeky.* These sentences are written in Burgess' characteristic style, but if you see the film you should remember that Kubrick directs according to his own style of film-making. Kubrick makes more of the attempted rape than Burgess does in the book and the film's fight scene is not as dance-like as the book's description. At the same time though, the film as a whole does convey a sense of Alex's enjoyment of violence, and this is particularly evident in the fight scene.

*S*tructure

The structure of the book, three parts of seven chapters each, is in keeping with its compressed, taut style. Characters and scenes that occur in the early part of the story recur, with and without some changes, in the later chapters. In Part 3 there are a number of telling echoes of earlier moments in the novel.

For instance, we have Alex once more entering the block of apartments where he used to live. However, there are small changes: the absence of graffiti and the working lifts indicate the passing of time. Alex returns to the music store, where he experiences a shock, and then the milkbar he used to frequent. This time he takes the kind of drug that he had once dismissed as *cowardly* and ends up resembling the type of person he contemptuously dismissed in the opening chapter of the book. The man he had attacked coming from the library in Part 1 recognizes him in the library in Part 3. These repetitions do more than register the passing of time; they also register the changed state of Alex and the consequences of his treatment.

As you read Part 3, be on the lookout for scenes and moments that echo an earlier part of the book. Throughout your reading, make a note of the dreams, including drug-induced ones, that are described. The author uses the idea of dreams to point ahead to what will happen and register significant moments in the story.

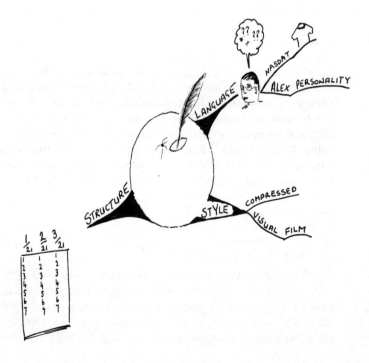

P*art 1*

Chapter 1

◆ Alex and his gang have a drink in a milk and drugs bar.
◆ They leave and attack and rob a man coming home from a library.
◆ An alibi is established by buying drinks for a group of older people in a pub.
◆ Disguised behind masks, Alex and his gang then attack and rob a shopkeeper and his wife before quickly returning to the pub.

The opening chapter begins in an ordinary enough setting, with a group of teenagers sitting one winter's evening in a milkbar wondering what they should do. However, Alex's vocabulary (see 'Language, style and structure' on p. 27) suggests that this is not the contemporary world, and the likelihood that the setting may be in the past – an American milkbar in the 1950s, say – is soon ruled out. The 'milk' is openly sold with various drugs while the dress codes of the teenagers in the milkbar are not part of any recognizable historical period. There are familiar aspects to the setting – a public library, a pub, street names, a police force – that make it recognizable as Britain, but the details indicate that we are in some future Britain where things have changed for the worse. Newspapers are not read much, libraries are rarely used, streets are not safe at night, milkbars dispense synthetic drugs that send their users into an unenlightened state of passive resignation, and the kind of violence that is acted out has a particularly nasty edge to it.

The special vocabulary of Alex and his *droogs* is the most obvious indication that they belong to a particular youth culture. It is a culture based around drug-taking, as the second paragraph makes clear, and the third paragraph shows how violent criminality is an everyday aspect of this subculture.

Following this, there are descriptions of the very visual dress costumes that characterize Alex's gang and the three girls in the milkbar. Like most youth cultures, the one that Alex and his type share belong to a particular social class. The man coming from the library that they attack belongs to the *older bourgeois type* and the girls in the milkbar wear wigs costing the equivalent of their monthly wages, suggesting that perhaps they do not earn a great deal.

This chapter's third paragraph introduces the theme of violence by way of Alex's automatic assumption that obtaining cash by robbery will involve an act of violence as well. His unquestioned attitude that violence is acceptable is expressed in the way he speaks (see the 'Language, style and structure' section below). Violence is more than just acceptable, it is to be welcomed, as the last words in this paragraph make clear. After just thinking that any need to obtain money will involve violence, and knowing that he has no cash shortage at the time, he then concludes that *as they say, money isn't everything*. The inference is that violence has an attraction regardless of the fact that there is no immediate need to obtain cash. This is borne out by the gratuitous attack on the man making his way home from the library. The second attack, on the shopkeeper and his wife, has a monetary motive but there is the same willing enjoyment of the violence it entails. ✪ Can violence be attractive? If so, in what way?

Just before leaving the milkbar, Alex observes the person sitting next to him who is lost in a drug-induced state. Alex, who used to take such drugs himself, now regards the kind of experience they offer as unsatisfactory. He rejects the spurious sense of reality they create and the passive lack of will that means *you lost your name and your body and your self and you just didn't care*. Alex's sense of independence and his wish to exercise his own will are revolted by a drug state that induces a feeling of helplessness and inaction. His own philosophy demands more freedom of will and he asserts that *you were not put on this earth just to get in touch with God* because he sees this as a passive role that will not exercise his own free will. Alex prefers another choice of drug, *milk with knives in it*, which acts as a stimulant and does not send him into a solipsistic trip in which contentment consists of being *hypnotised by your boot or shoe*.

The fact that Alex gratuitously hits the drugged young man before leaving the milkbar may indicate his strength of feeling about the surrender of one's free will in the way that he describes. ✪ Read this paragraph again, beginning *The chelloveck sitting next to me,* and underline phrases that point to Alex's sense that free will is important.

The end of this chapter has Alex complaining about the lack of challenge in outwitting the police, *nothing to fight against really,* confirming the idea that Alex has a will of his own and that he feels discontent at the poor opportunities awaiting someone with his sense of initiative and autonomy.

LANGUAGE, STYLE AND STRUCTURE

Start as you mean to go on and begin compiling your *nasdat* dictionary from the outset. To help get you going, all the *nasdat* words from the first couple of paragraphs, in the order they occur, are given below. You should keep your dictionary in alphabetical order, inserting new words as and when they occur.

droogs friends	*horrorshow* good, well
rassoodocks mind	*mozg* brain
flip wild	*deng* money
mesto place	*crasting* robbing
skorry quickly	*pretty polly* money
prodding producing	*tolchock* hit, beat
veshches things	*veck* (from *chelloveck*) person, male
moloko milk	
peet drink (verb)	*viddy* see (verb)
vellocet a drug	*starry* very old
synthemesc a drug	*ptitsa* young woman
drencrom a drug	*smecking* laughing

Burgess goes beyond just inventing a set of new words and scattering them amongst Alex's monologues and dialogues. Alex uses language in a highly expressive way and his attitude is often revealed by the way he speaks. In the third paragraph, when dismissing any need to rob someone, he speaks of there being no need *to tolchock some old veck in an alley and viddy him swim in his blood while we counted the takings and divided by four.* The choice of words and the casual tone express his unwillingness or inability to empathize with the sufferings of others. Later, in the attack on the man with the library books, *out comes the blood, my brothers, real beautiful* and when Alex attacks the woman in the shop it *brought the red out like an old friend.* The way Alex speaks brings out his enjoyment of violence. His apparent inability to connect blood with suffering and pain may point to a fundamental inadequacy on his part. ✪ How far do you think his callous behaviour is caused by the dystopian society in which he has been brought up?

Chapter 2

◆ Alex and his gang violently attack an old drunk on the street.
◆ A fight with Billyboy's gang is interrupted by the arrival of the police.
◆ Alex and his gang attack the residents of a country cottage and the woman occupant is gang-raped.

Like the man coming home from the library, the drunk outside the Duke of New York (Is the pub name a little joke by Burgess about the increasing Americanization of British culture?) is another helpless victim of the gang's liking for violent attacks on complete strangers. This time there is not even the semblance of a robbery, although the motive that gives rise to the attack is interesting. ✪ Re-read the first paragraph and underline the sentence that suggests a reason for the attack on the man. Alex feels provoked to attack by the sad state of the man and what gets to him is the man's drunkenness and his indifference to his appearance and behaviour. This could tie in with Alex's aggressive dismissal of the drugged man in the milkbar, who also annoyed him because of the way he abandoned his will to the power of the drug. The drug in question this time is alcohol but its debilitating effect is seen by Alex as similar to the synthetic drugs added to the drinks in the Korova Milkbar.

On a register of violent outrage, the attack on the drunk comes second to the attack on the cottage in this chapter. Alex and his gang are intent on causing as much damage as they can, with *lashings of ultra-violence,* and this time their enjoyment is less apparent. Alex says himself that *we were full of hate* and they vandalize the cottage interior with a venomous spirit of destruction.

This chapter's two very violent encounters, the gang fight and the attack on the cottage residents, raise the theme of crime and punishment. The drunk man on the pavement complains about the lack of law and order and what is seen of the police suggests they are fighting a losing battle. The lack of law and order, at this stage in the novel, is seen as an aspect of a breakdown in society and it prepares the ground for the government's response that will be made clear in future chapters of the novel.

Alex likes to *slooshy* (to hear) what some of his victims say about life and this drunk's remarks reinforce the idea that the culture and society of *A Clockwork Orange* is a dystopian one. The man pessimistically exclaims at the gulf between what technology has achieved in outer space and the kind of lawless society that exists down on earth. The man's mood could be explained away as sentimental pieties from a hopeless drunk, but what he says is borne out by what we have seen so far of the society in which he dwells, and not least the unprovoked way in which he is beaten up. **✪** Look back at the account of the older women in the Duke of New York pub in Chapter 1 and ask yourself whether you think they would agree with the drunk.

This chapter confirms the earlier evidence of the novel's dystopian society. Everyday violence seems to be taken for granted, at least by the youth subculture, and one of the more shocking incidents illustrating this is the scene involving the little girl who is inadvertently saved when Alex's gang first come across Billyboy and his associates (see p. 31). This confirms the fact that the violent behaviour of Alex and his gang is not uncharacteristic of youth gangs in this society. The police are armed, for they arrive on the scene *with pooshkas* [guns] *pushing out of the police-auto-windows.*

In our age of live satellite transmissions around the world, it may be a little unsettling to realize that Burgess imagined such a phenomenon forty years ago as another aspect of a dystopian future. When Alex talks of *a worldcast* television show seen simultaneously all over the world, it becomes part of the novel's frightening society where one section of people, *mostly the middle-aged middle-class*, watch satellite television while another section roam the streets seeking violence as their choice of leisure activity or lapse into drugged oblivion in a milkbar. There seems to be an alarming lack of choices but Dim, at the end of this paragraph describing them resting in an alleyway surrounded by flashes of blue light from the countless television sets, looks up at the stars in imaginative wonder. ✪ Is this a way of emphasizing the spiritual poverty of the culture? Why do you think the author has Dim asking a not-so-dim question?

The description of the encounter between the rival gangs of Alex and Billyboy makes it plain that such gangs are fairly common. The way both sides eye each other up and prepare for a fight also makes it clear that such violent encounters are not unusual. Alex relishes the prospect of a serious fight involving the *nozh* (knife), the *oozy* (chain) and the *britva* (razor) and there is no indication that Billyboy and his associates feel very different.

The significance of the novel's title is introduced in this chapter (see 'Themes' section of this guide, under 'Free will'), and it is interesting that the author chooses to do so in a scene that illustrates the ugliest and least palatable side to the exercise of free will. *A Clockwork Orange* will argue that, ultimately, respect must be accorded to the notion of a person's capacity for free will and that to remove this ability can be regarded as a crime against humanity. By choosing to introduce this idea in a scene of rape and violence it may be that the author wishes to emphasize that he is under no illusions about just how unacceptable human behaviour can become. In the abstract, a person may indeed be *a creature of growth and capable of sweetness* but there is no evidence of this in the barbaric behaviour of Alex and his gang at the cottage. ✪ Does this mean that the author is contradicting himself? If the exercise of free will can result in brutal rape and violence why is it wrong to impose a mechanical restraint? One possible response to this would arise out of an awareness that people do not act in a social or political vacuum and that material circumstances may help explain why people sometimes act the way they do. The dystopian nature of the novel's society suggests that the author is well aware of this and that he wants the reader to judge Alex in the context of the dysfunctional world he inhabits.

When Alex comes across the drunk in the street he says how he liked to *slooshy what some of these starry decreps had to say about life and the world*. Alex has curiosity and his interest in listening to what other people have to say raises the possibility that he is capable of change. This only becomes obvious much later in the story, but it is worth noting how here, very early on in the novel, we see Alex as a young person who is curious about the world.

LANGUAGE, STYLE AND STRUCTURE

Alex's individual personality expresses itself in his personal **idiom**, whether insulting a rival – *How art thou, thou globby bottle of cheap stinking chip-oil?* – or describing his own behaviour, as when he compares his movement with the razor as being like a barber on a boat in a rough sea. His description of the fight with Billyboy confirms the earlier impression that he actively enjoys violence. Behind his graphic use of **simile** (*like two curtains of blood*) and **metaphor** (his movement as a *waltz*) lies a mind that sees the effect of his violence in purely visual terms. Alex enjoys the drama of the fight and no questions of right and wrong arise in his mind.

The description of the gang fight raises the question of how the reader responds to depictions of violence as seen from Alex's point of view. When Alex says *Dim had a real horrorshow length of oozy* or *this droog of Billyboy's went tottering off and howling his heart out*, the speaker brings his own enjoyment of the scene into the language. The victim of Dim's swinging metal chain has been caught around the face by it, but the viciousness of the attack or the painful plight of the victim is not evoked. This is because Alex does not comprehend the fight in these terms and the author does not present another point of view. Then again, you might say, the author is not under any obligation to do so. The more important point is that Alex's use of language reflects the way he experiences the fight, and his point of view is communicated to the reader through the language. Phrases like *tottering off* and *howling his heart out* might be appropriate to describe the antics of hapless, digitally rendered victims after being targeted and destroyed in a violent, fantasy computer game. Violence to Alex is a game, full of excitement and unpredictability.

This aspect to the novel's language arises again in the description of the violent rape scene in the cottage. ✪ Does the style of this passage seem similar to you or do you think it also conveys a sense of outrage at what is taking place? Try to find actual words and phrases on which to base your opinion.

Chapter 3

- ◆ Alex and the gang return to the Korova Milkbar.
- ◆ Alex hits Dim and causes resentment within the gang.
- ◆ Returning home, Alex listens to some of his favourite classical music.

By the end of this chapter the reader has some more details regarding Alex's environment, and the overall picture of society being presented is a fairly depressing one. Alex lives on the tenth floor of a block of flats, where he seems unsurprised by the fact that the lift has been vandalized: in this area gang fights and other acts of violence are common. The badly polluted canal on the outskirts of town and the painting of a proletarian scene in his block of flats suggest that Alex lives in an industrial, working-class environment. The middle-class cottage from Chapter 2 is situated in the countryside outside the town, suggesting that the social classes are clearly divided and demarcated. Even though there are some professional people in the milkbar, Alex notes that they were *not of the bourgeois, never them*. The food left at home for Alex by his parents, *lomticks* (pieces) *of tinned spongemeat with a shive* (slice) *or so of kleb* (bread) *and butter*, suggests they probably live on a meagre budget.

Central to the dystopian vision of *A Clockwork Orange* is the ubiquitous presence of violent and dysfunctional behaviour in everyday life. Alex's gang vandalize the train interior because they are unable to relax for even a three-minute journey. Alex strikes out at Dim in the milkbar as if this is his automatic response to any displeasure and he shows no surprise, let alone any thought of offering assistance, when he comes across an injured girl (a *malchick*) near his block of flats, the victim of another violent attack.

Alex himself, as he listens to some of his favourite music at home, indulges in a sadistic sexual fantasy whereby he imagines himself grinding his boot in the faces of helpless victims and committing acts of sexual violence. He seems to appreciate the music for its own sake but the satisfaction he gains from listening to it is disturbingly linked with his enjoyment of thoughts of sexual violence.

Readers are sometimes surprised to discover, in the opening sentence of this chapter's second paragraph, that Alex and his gang are still at school. He lives at home with his parents, who prepare his meals and his favourite activity, *pride of my jeezny* (life), is listening to music in his bedroom. He is only 15. This may seem shocking, considering what he gets up to in the evenings, and it also raises the question of how far he can be held responsible for what he does. ✪ Does it make any difference if someone committing acts of violence and rape is an adolescent rather than an adult?

Alex belongs to a gang and shares the ethos of a youth culture, but his strong sense of individuality and his own personal values cause problems. Chapter 3 shows tensions developing within Alex's gang, prompted by him hitting Dim for being rude to the female singer in the milkbar. Alex's behaviour threatens the group identity because of the way he aggressively asserts his leadership. It is clear that Georgie and Pete are on Dim's side and although they all part on friendly terms it seems that Alex is in danger of isolating himself within the group.

The theme of free will in the novel is closely linked with the individual personality of Alex. Alex is differentiated from Dim, Pete and Georgie, and the reader is closer to his thoughts and feelings than those of any other character in the story. By the end of Chapter 3, Alex has emerged as a complex and interesting character even though he has raped someone and violently attacked a number of innocent people. Alex is quite unlike the individual who is still in a drugged state of oblivion when he and his gang return to the Korova Milkbar. That person is described as having a *pale inhuman look, like he'd become a thing, and like his litso* [face] *was really a piece of chalk, carved.* No such lack of expression characterizes Alex when he hears and recognizes a bar and a half from an opera he likes. The music almost changes his personality, causing him to chastise Dim for a lack of manners in reacting rudely to the woman singing. The shock registered by Dim at this charge is probably shared by most readers who react with incredulity to the idea that Alex should be offended by a show of bad manners.

The importance of the role of music in Alex's life is emphasized by the author in the detailed account he gives of the way it affects the young hooligan. *Oh, it was gorgeousness and gorgeosity made flesh*, exclaims Alex who becomes quite lyrical in his choice of images to describe the heavenly effect that the music has on him (see 'Language, style and structure' section below). ✪ In the penultimate paragraph, beginning *Then, brothers, it came*, underline the images and metaphors that Alex uses to describe the music.

Alex's ability to appreciate classical music may seem extraordinary. Here is a dangerously violent delinquent responding passionately to the music of Plautus, Mozart and Bach. His creative use of language to describe the music is a reflection of its powerful effect on him. An important question is beginning to emerge about Alex. Is his delinquency a result of his social environment whereas his sophisticated appreciation of music indicates a highly interesting personality? ✪ What do you think?

Note how this chapter ends. Alex recalls seeing the term 'a clockwork orange' in the writer's work in the cottage and feels that listening to the music of Bach helps him understand what the term means. We know (see p. 15) that the term relates to the theme of free will and presumably something along these lines occurs to Alex as he enjoys the music. Yet the last sentence in this chapter has Alex concluding that, given his new understanding of the idea of a clockwork orange, he only wishes he had inflicted more violence on the writer and his wife. ✪ There is no obvious right answer to this question, but why do you think Alex reacts in this way after thinking about the idea of a clockwork orange?

LANGUAGE, STYLE AND STRUCTURE

The paragraph beginning *Then, brothers, it came* conveys the heightened joy that Alex experiences when listening to his favourite classical music. His choice of images – *silverflamed* trumpets, *like rarest spun heavenmetal, like a cage of silk around my bed* – are not just thrown together for some aggregate of lyricism. The music of each instrument in the piece is described in turn and with precision, so that the piercing oboe and flute, for example, are like *worms of platinum,* whereas the soft, fluid sound of the violin is like *silvery wine flowing in a spaceship, gravity all nonsense now.* Alex takes a genuine delight in his music and his description reveals a finesse and a sensibility that is at odds with his brutal and violent behaviour patterns.

Now viddy (look at) this

? Part of Alex's individuality expresses itself in his fussiness about food manners, personal appearance and hygiene. Some examples have already been given (see 'Characterization' section, under 'Alex') but try to find another example from the end of Chapter 2 and another one from the beginning of Chapter 3.

? Make notes for a Mini Mind Map to show the similarities and differences between your society and the one presented in the first three chapters of *A Clockwork Orange.*

? Match up the *nasdat* words on the left with the meanings on the right. They all come from the sixth paragraph in Chapter 1.

devotchkas	buying
rotyoung	girls
kupetting	mouth
gulliver	head
pol	eyes
sharps	girls
glazzies	slept
spatted	sex

? These *nasdat* words occur in Chapter 3. Try to work out their meanings:

yeckated, sobiratted, rozzes, carmen, platties, fillying, von, malenky, cheenas, krovvy, yarbles, razdraz, bezoomy, spatchka, neezhnies, plott, klootch, moloko, radrezzed.

(Answers on p. 80)

Now have a break — try slooshying (listening to) some good music (it could even be some Bach!).

Chapter 4

◆ Alex dreams of losing authority to Georgie and Dim.
◆ His probation officer makes a short visit.
◆ Alex picks up two young girls and invites them back to his home.

The reader finds out a little more about Alex's home environment. Both his parents work, his father in a dyeworks and his mother in a supermarket stacking shelves. This confirms the earlier impression of Alex's working-class environment and the fact that materially they are not very well off. We also find out that a law has been passed making work compulsory for everyone except pregnant mothers or those with young children. The newspaper that Alex reads suggests a society in conflict with industrial disputes and high crime rates, and footballers threatening not to play over a pay dispute.

Alex mentioned his attendance at *corrective schools* towards the end of the previous chapter and P. R. Deltoid is a probation officer responsible for monitoring the boy's behaviour and hopefully keeping him on the right side of the law. Deltoid, however, seems resigned to the fact that Alex has not changed his criminal nature and he shows little interest in trying to help. In Kubrick's film, Deltoid is quite successfully presented as a sarcastic and not very salubrious adult who has clearly become cynical about his job. What he does do is ask the fundamental question about the cause of Alex's criminality: *What gets into you all? ... a good home here, good loving parents ... is it some devil that crawls inside you?* Deltoid is not being serious in suggesting some kind of demonic possession, but the far-fetched idea does show how far he is from understanding what might be the cause of behaviour like that of Alex and his gang. ◗ To what extent is it true to say that Alex has a good home? From what you have seen of Alex's home life and his environment, do you share Deltoid's amazement about how it could produce criminal behaviour?

Alex offers his own thoughts on the cause of his criminality, in the second half of the paragraph beginning *But when he'd ookadeeted* (left). He chooses to act badly because at this stage in his life he enjoys it. He says that the prospect of imprisonment will prove a strong deterrent but until that eventuality arrives he is happy to go on the way he is. Acting in a bad or a good way is a matter of choice, he reasons, and so *badness is of the self, the one, the you or me.* He says that a person's free will accounts for how they behave and he goes on to argue that the authorities *cannot allow the bad because they cannot allow the self.* Indeed, he claims, recent history is full of struggles between individual will and the forces of control. Alex is suggesting that his society, any society perhaps, seeks to enforce conformity by controlling the way individuals express themselves. Forces of control, like the government and schools, react negatively to expressions of individuality. ◗ To what extent, if any, do you agree with Alex's analysis? Whether you agree with Alex or not, his thoughts about the causes of his criminality indicate his intelligence and powers of thinking. He is able to reflect on issues and articulate thoughts at an abstract level.

The girls in the record shop represent another example of youth culture in the novel's society. They are younger than Alex but dress to look older, with *padded groodies* (breasts) and lipstick, and have their own type of music and language (see 'Language, style and structure' below).

An example of the way in which some of the novel's themes overlap may be found in the section where Alex sarcastically dismisses newspaper discussions about youth culture. Issues of parental discipline, shortage of teachers, and the responsibility of adults in creating an unsafe world are raised as possible causes of the problems within youth culture. These issues touch on the themes of crime and punishment, violence and dystopia in the novel.

Ironically, Alex laughs at these issues and asks sarcastically: *So we young innocent malchicks could take no blame. Right right right.* He laughs because in his opinion they all ignore what he has previously admitted, namely that he chooses out of his own free will to act the way he does. As if to demonstrate the point, Alex brings home two impressionable young girls, fills them with alcohol and, with the help of other drugs that he takes himself, subjects them to sexual violence while stirred on by Beethoven's *Ninth Symphony*. It is a brutal rejoinder to the author of the newspaper article suggesting that a better Arts education would have a civilizing effect on modern youth. Any solution to the problems created by the dystopian society of *A Clockwork Orange* will have to be more complex than this.

 ## LANGUAGE, STYLE AND STRUCTURE

Who you getten, bratty? What biggy, what only? Even Alex, an experienced speaker of *nasdat*, is not familiar with the language of the two young girls in the record shop. The fact that they also have their own kind of music reinforces the idea that in this society different groups are separating themselves within the community through cultural markers like language and music. To some extent, of course, this has always been the case in society, but in this novel Burgess is taking it a stage further and imagining the process as part of a fracturing in the social order.

Kubrick's film of the novel handles the scene with the two girls in a style that is different to the book. The sexual encounter is presented with speeded-up film of repetitive, quick-fire motions of undressing and dressing in Alex's bedroom. The general sense is that of casual and voluntary sex, whereas the book dwells more on the predatory nature of Alex and the nastiness of his inclination for sexual violence. Burgess is not trying to avoid the unpleasant consequences of people like Alex feeling free to indulge themselves.

Chapter 5

◆ Alex converses with his father at home.
◆ Alex fights Georgie and Dim for challenging his authority.
◆ They seem to make friends and plan a more ambitious robbery.

This chapter starts with a family at home sitting down to an evening meal. The domestic setting, and the father's well-meaning concern for his son, is a reminder that Alex is a young teenager with parents who have little understanding of him. His parents come across as rather weak-minded compared to the assertive will of their son, and Alex is adept at keeping them in ignorance. Given that Alex has attended corrective schools and been in trouble with the police before now, there is a suggestion that his parents have given up trying to influence him. ❂ Can you recall how his mother responded when Alex gave his excuse for not getting up for school, in the previous chapter? Alex is growing up with little understanding from his parents but he seems unbothered by it.

Georgie is also growing up and it shows in his willingness to challenge Alex's leadership of the gang and his suggestion that they raise the level of their criminal activities. Alex deals with this new situation by first attacking Georgie in the street and then taking on Dim. Relying on his intuition, Alex feels that this is the best way to deal with what he sees as a threat to his authority. It seems to work because, once the fighting is over, it appears that all is well once more between Alex and his *droogs*. The source of the discord within the gang lies with Alex's treatment of Dim and, more generally, a desire on the part of Georgie and the others to raise the level of their criminal behaviour and take on more ambitious and financially lucrative robberies. Alex, by comparison, seems content with the haphazard and spontaneous kind of criminality that they have normally practised. Georgie is attracted by the idea of becoming a professional criminal whereas Alex seems happy with the way things are.
❂ What does this suggest about the kind of person Alex is?

Chapter 6

◆ Alex and his gang plan to rob a house called the Manse.
◆ The plan goes wrong and Alex is attacked by Dim and left to be picked up by the police.

There have been various indications that all is not well within Alex's gang and matters come to a head in this chapter. Alex thinks he is being the magnanimous leader by agreeing to Georgie's idea of robbing the Manse but he insists on being in charge of the attempted ruse to gain entry to the house. When this fails, he takes it upon himself to break in and then decides to show his leadership qualities once he is inside the house. Dim, however, has not forgotten his recent treatment at the hands of Alex and gets his revenge. The youth culture that Alex, Georgie, Dim and Pete shared has come to an inglorious end.

LANGUAGE, STYLE AND STRUCTURE

Part 1 of the novel is drawing to a conclusion and the author has prepared the ground beforehand by way of the gang's dissension and by the structural device of characters' dreams. In Chapter 2, Alex had a dream about his subjection at the hands of Pete and Dim and in the following chapter his father's dream shows his son fallen and beaten by fellow gang members. Chapter 5 sees the relevance of these dreams played out in the fractured relationship between Alex and his *droogs*. Chapter 6 begins in a familiar enough way, but there is a hint of continuing conflict within the group when Georgie questions Alex's plan for the break-in. The almost farcical struggle between Alex and the woman distracts the reader's attention so that there is an element of dramatic surprise when the door is opened and Dim is waiting with his chain.
✪ Are you as surprised as Alex to find Dim there?

Chapter 7

◆ Alex is beaten up by the police, and P. R. Deltoid spits in his face.
◆ Alex, placed in a cell with other prisoners, seeks solace by dreaming of Beethoven's music.
◆ Alex learns that the woman he attacked has died and that he now faces a more severe punishment.

Until now, most of the story has concerned itself with the criminal activities of Alex and his gang. Having been caught by the police, Alex is about to experience the world of punishment and in one way there is no great change except that Alex is now on the receiving end of the violence. He first hears the sound of someone being *tolchocked* (beaten) in their cell and it is not long before Alex receives a systematic beating from the police. Alex is not surprised by being beaten, but what does come as a surprise is Deltoid's behaviour towards him. ✪ Why do you think Alex expresses no surprise at being beaten up by the police?

The police officer, in offering a lame excuse to Deltoid for beating Alex, says that *violence makes violence*. Apart from the fact that this is not strictly true in Alex's case, the officer would seem to be expressing a more general observation that Alex deserves what he gets because it is his violent behaviour that has provoked the police response. ✪ Can you see the weakness in the police officer's defence of beating Alex?

Part of the novel's dystopian vision is that law and order has broken down, not just in the sense that there is a lot of criminal behaviour but also in the way that the police and the probation service are themselves part of the problem. The police also take violence for granted and, like Alex and his gang, practise it in their own work as a matter of course. The police invite Deltoid to do the same, although he prefers to show his feelings by spitting in Alex's face. ✪ Why do you think he does this? Is it because he just dislikes Alex and wants to express his frustrated rage at the way the system is failing to cope with criminals, or is it annoyance at the way his own career prospects will be dented by Alex's failure to reform? Perhaps it is both at the same time, but what is sure is that the system of crime and punishment does not seem to be working very well.

The themes of violence and crime and punishment come together in the dystopian description of Alex's night in the prison cell. It is a very depressing picture of a society's ills, with no suggestion that prison will deal with problems of crime and violence. The reader can almost share Alex's relief at being transported in his sleep *to another better world* where Beethoven's *Ninth* offers comfort. The reality of the next morning brings more bad news and Alex is left to contemplate his fate. *That was everything. I'd done the lot, now. And me still only fifteen.* Alex's age has been kept back until this moment and it comes as a dramatic surprise to discover that he is not an adult.

Alex has always been differentiated from the other members of his gang by his concern with personal habits and appearance, and there are a few examples in this chapter. He feels *dismay* at the poor state of his physical appearance in the police station and notices in detail personal aspects of the policeman who first hits him. When he is being hit, he seems more worried about getting whitewash from the walls onto his clothes than about the physical punishment being administered. His apology for vomiting is heartfelt because this is not the way he likes to behave in public. Alex is not vain but he has always taken pride in his appearance and he finds it difficult to retain his sense of dignity in the police station.

LANGUAGE, STYLE AND STRUCTURE

Alex's crimes, and his punishment at the hands of the police, have been adult in nature and this adds to the dramatic effect of the chapter's final sentence. Within the structure of the novel as a whole this is a key moment because it comes as the conclusion to Part 1 of the novel. It is not a complete surprise because the reader already knew he was still attending school, and domestic moments with his family emphasized his adolescence, but there is a shock value attached to the last sentence. The incidents of rape, sadistic violence and police brutality have all been about a 15-year-old boy, not some hardened professional criminal. Moreover, mainly through the language he uses to express himself, Alex comes across as someone with a strong sense of individuality. Having all this happen to him by the age of 15 leaves the reader wondering what is in store for Alex. It is a highly effective and dramatic end to the first part of the novel.

Put your rassoodock (mind) to this

? Check your knowledge of *nasdat* by giving meanings to the following words:

Chapter 4: *sneety, govoreeting, choodrssny, zammechat*. Chapter 5: *carman, nochy, itty, cutter, shilarney, gloopy, goloss, odin dva tree*. Chapter 6: *bolshy, domies, dorogoy, zvonock, oddy knocky, nogas, kots and koshkas, grahzny, bratchnies, gorloes*. Chapter 7: *plennies, zvook, strack, gromky, brooko, merzky, bugatty, shiyah, oozhassny, shoom*. (Answers on p. 80)

? Find a quote from Chapters 4–7 to support each of these statements. See if your teacher agrees with you:

> P. R. Deltoid has no faith that Alex will stay out of trouble.
> Alex's parents have given up trying to influence him.
> Alex is determined to assert his leadership over the gang.

? The following list covers seven key moments, one from each chapter of Part 1, but they are in random order, not the order in which they occur. Try reordering them without looking at the novel and then check your answer. Make any necessary corrections so that you end up with a list in the correct order.

> **A**lex is in heaven when he listens to a violin concerto by Plautus.
> **A** fight within the gang reveals tensions between Alex and his *droogs*.
> **I**t is one of Alex's victims who uses the term 'clockwork orange'.
> **C**ats get in the way of Alex before he is surprised by Dim.
> **O**nly a dream of Beethoven's music keeps Alex's spirits up when detained in a prison cell overnight.
> **L**ittle affection exists between Alex and P. R. Deltoid.
> **H**anging out in the milkbar, Alex introduces himself and his gang.

A possible mnemonic for the correct sequence could be: **H**ow **i**s **A**lex **l**ike **a** **c**lockwork **o**range?

Your plott (body) deserves a rest – take a break.

Part 2

Chapter 1

- ◆ Alex has been in prison for two years.
- ◆ One of his jobs is helping the prison chaplain.
- ◆ Alex asks about Ludovico's Technique, a new method of treatment.

The idea of a prisoner being identified by a number, and not a name, is commonplace, but nonetheless it serves to introduce the key change in Alex's situation: *I was 6655321 and not your little droog Alex not no longer*. A prisoner of the state, he can only reminisce with himself over the days when he *was like happy and free*. A piece of good fortune leads to Alex's duties in the prison chapel and, by playing up to the chaplain's hopes that he has a born-again Christian to nurture, he has opportunities to listen to some of his favourite music.

When Alex prods the chaplain about the mysterious Ludovico's Technique – a method that attracts Alex because it involves a release from prison – the chaplain confesses to having doubts about its morality. At this stage the reader is unaware of how this new method works but the chaplain knows about it and he questions whether it can really make someone good. *Goodness is something chosen. When a man cannot choose he ceases to be a man.* The significance of this remark, which goes to the heart of the book's ethical message, will only become apparent later.

What is known at this stage is that Alex still chooses to pursue what gives him pleasure and this does not fit the traditional category of goodness. He enjoys reading the Old Testament because of its stories involving violence and sex, but the New Testament, covering the life and death of Christ, has less immediate appeal for him. ○ Identify the passage in the book where Alex identifies with tales from the Old Testament. When he is persuaded to read the New Testament, the story of Christ's crucifixion catches his imagination because he finds himself attracted to *helping in and even taking charge of the tolchocking and the nailing in, being dressed in a like toga*. Alex enjoys the prospect of inflicting violence and, characteristically, the toga dress appeals to his sense of clothes vanity. This blasphemous engagement with the Bible seems to signal the complete irrelevance of Christian notions to the world of Alex and *A Clockwork Orange*. Looking ahead to what will be Alex's fate in prison, there may be some irony in his fascination with the crucifixion of Christ because Alex himself will be 'crucified' by the state as a kind of sacrificial lamb.

The prison environment is often portrayed in novels as a dispiriting place and Staja is no exception. The prison routine sounds familiar enough but a dystopian note is added by having the guards carry guns. ✪ Do you remember where the reader finds out the police are armed as well? (See p. 29 of this guide.) The idea of prison overcrowding is not new either but the author draws attention to this aspect in the last paragraph of the chapter. ✪ To which of the novel's themes does this paragraph relate? The rise in the prison population has doubled the number of prisoners in the cells and the rate of incarceration is increasing: *it's going to get worse, not better. A right dirty criminal world you lot are trying to build.* Apart from the fact that this statement contributes to the general spirit of dystopia that characterizes the world in which Alex is growing up, it also touches on the theme of crime and punishment. Whatever else the prison experience might achieve, it is not lowering the crime rate.

LANGUAGE, STYLE AND STRUCTURE

Alex, as well as being a character in his own right, has the structural role of narrator and this comes to the fore in the first couple of pages of this chapter. The second paragraph condenses the story of Alex's life from where Part 1 ended to his present sojourn in Staja, while the fourth paragraph relates the death of Georgie. This effects a smooth transition so that the narrative can continue with the reader acquainted with the passing of time over two years and aware of significant little changes in Alex's situation.

Alex, of course, is far more than the voice of the narrator. The ideas that are explored through the novel's themes are embodied in Alex's experiences and of primary importance in this respect is Alex's use of language. Look, for example, at the sixth paragraph, beginning *I was in the Wing Chapel*. The author does not use Alex as a mere mouthpiece for delivering a discourse on the poor quality of prison life and the importance of free will. Instead, Alex describes the scene as he sees it, and through his language the reader shares his dismay at the *bolshy blue brutal jowls* of the wardens guarding the churchgoers with their rifles. Alex's perception that his will is being sapped in prison is expressed in his characteristic awareness of body odour, this time the *dusty, greasy, hopeless sort of a von* of the prisoners. The key word here is *hopeless*, and, even more significantly, Alex realizes that he too is beginning to acquire this prison odour. Alex is aware of the threat to his free will if he remains in prison. In the physical sense, of course, prison obviously limits the free will of the prisoners, but Alex is referring here to a possible loss of his free will in a deeper sense. ✪ Explain in your own words what Alex is worried about if he remains a prisoner.

Try this

❔ Check that you have noted the following words, listed in their order of appearance in Chapter 1. (Answers on p. 80.)

> *raskazz, slovos, prestoopnicks, groody, ded, bezoony, millicents, grazzy, yahoodies, pischa, privodeeted.*

Chapter 2

◆ Alex's cell becomes even more overcrowded with the arrival of another prisoner.
◆ The new prisoner is attacked and dies of his injuries.
◆ Alex is selected by a government minister for a new course of treatment.

The previous chapter was set entirely in the prison and this chapter narrows the focus still more and takes place entirely in a prison cell. The theme of crime and punishment comes to the fore and the issues raised are surprisingly relevant to our contemporary world. Little of what takes place in the cell seems to belong to some imagined, futuristic prison. The overcrowding, the forcing together of prisoners that should be kept apart, unsympathetic guards, the violence that always threatens to erupt, are all familiar aspects of reports about prison life today. As the government minister points out, prisons bring together a concentration of criminality and this overrides whatever else prisons might be trying to achieve. In the early 1960s, when Burgess was writing, the kind of pessimism expressed by the minister would have been more shocking. This is one example of the way the dystopian society of *A Clockwork Orange* makes contact with our world today, suggesting that Burgess was prescient about the way some aspects of his world were developing.

Another dystopian note is added towards the end of the chapter when the government minister remarks that *soon we may be needing all our prison space for political offenders.* The whole idea of political prisoners runs against the grain of a liberal democratic society which practises freedom of expression. Unless a criminal offence has been committed for a political cause, people are not supposed to go to prison because of their political beliefs. It is not clear what kind of *offences* the minister has in mind but he does draw a distinction between criminals and the kind of prisoner he thinks the prisons may be needed for. ✪ What kind of political offences do you think the author may have had in mind?

The fact that violence in prison is taken for granted is itself an ironical comment on the idea that criminals can be reformed by spending time in prison. The overnight incident in Alex's cell not only confirms how widespread violence is in the society of *A Clockwork Orange*, but it also confirms how difficult it will be to do anything effective about it. The minister's observation that prisoners *enjoy their so-called punishment* seems to be borne out by Alex's reaction to the sight of blood as the new prisoner is beaten up by his cellmates: *seeing the old krovvy* [blood] *flow red in the red light, I felt the old joy like rising up in my keeshkas* [guts]. However, this does not mean that the minister is right in saying that prisoners enjoy their time inside. Even though Alex enjoys the sight of blood, the prison experience as a whole is portrayed in very dismal terms. ✪ What aspect of prison life, as presented in this chapter, do you find most depressing?

Try this

? These are new *nasdat* words that appear in this chapter. Check your understanding of their meanings against the answers on p. 80.

nachinatted, zasnoot, sloochatted, podooshka, keeshkas, oobivat

Chapter 3

◆ Alex signs a form agreeing to a new course of treatment.
◆ The chaplain expresses his ethical doubts about the treatment.
◆ Alex innocently looks forward to his treatment.

This chapter explores the implications of the remark made by the politician at the end of the previous chapter. *Kill the criminal reflex*, he announced, after speaking of the need for a *curative* approach to the problem of crime. The governor, believing in the maxim of 'an eye for an eye', advocates a more traditional approach to the problem. His idea, that violence should be met with violence, was stated earlier in the novel by another character. ✪ Can you remember who this character was and what the situation was? (Look in Chapter 7 of Part 1 if you are not sure.) The governor's theory has the severe drawback that, far from reducing crime, it only fuels the problem. The government, acknowledging this difficulty, has come up with a new possible solution. This, however, has its own problems, which are articulated by the prison chaplain.

As we have seen in the 'Characterization' section of this guide, the chaplain serves more as a mouthpiece for a particular ethical point of view than as a complex character in his own right. Faced with a method of brainwashing that will abolish freedom of choice but remove the propensity for violence, he comes down in favour of the primacy of free will. He poses the question of whether free will is so essential a part of being human that to remove it completely constitutes a serious ethical crime. He asks whether a man who chooses to be bad is *perhaps in some way better* than someone who is forced against his will to be good. ✪ What do you take the word *better* to mean in this sentence? He is not better in the eyes of the law, and the victim of a violent crime would probably feel justified in thinking this was an odd way of putting it.

The chaplain, however, is not addressing the problem in these terms. At an ethical and philosophical level, the ability to make a moral choice is inseparable from being a moral person, from being a human being. To think in terms of making choices, exercising one's free will is to rise above the level of a machine, to rise above being a clockwork orange. From this point of view, being good because one has been programmed in this way is to be robbed of one's humanity. This is what the chaplain means when he says – and this is a quotation worth memorizing – that *It may not be nice to be good, little 6655321. It may be horrible to be good.*

Bound up with the theme of free will at this stage, Alex's naivety and lack of experience become very apparent in this chapter. He is, remember, only 17 years old and has gone from a criminal youth gang to an adult prison. He has virtually no experience of the world outside of his youth culture and then prison, and is vulnerable to exploitation because of this. This, after all, is what happened to him in the previous chapter. In his talk with the chaplain, Alex also reveals limited comprehension of the situation he is about to enter. Alex dismisses what the chaplain is saying, partly because the chaplain is obviously getting drunk, and partly because he simply doesn't comprehend the nature of the treatment to which he has just signed his agreement. It is because of this lack of understanding that he fails to see the significance of the chaplain's alcohol-fuelled remarks. Another example of Alex's naivety is his encounter with Dr Branom. The young Alex is too easily taken in by the doctor's conventional niceties and fondly wonders whether *it will be just like going to the pictures?* He also imagines that he will soon be able to return to his gang and take up his own life. Alex hasn't changed a great deal and his youthful inexperience allows him to think he will be unaffected by his Pavlovian treatment. ✪ Identify a passage or two, towards the end of this chapter, where Alex betrays his innocent lack of awareness of anything sinister or worrying about his situation.

The attitude of the governor, and of the police officer who condoned the beating up of Alex in the police station, is part of the problem of violence. It is not a solution to the problem because, to judge from the severely overcrowded prisons, the crime rate has not decreased. Nor is it clear which came first – the violence of young people like Alex or the institutionalized violence of the police and the prison system. The ineffectiveness of institutionalized violence as a means of controlling individual violence is brought out at the start of this chapter when Alex is casually hit by *brutal tolchocking chassos* (guards) on his way to the governor and then *tolchocked on the back and the gulliver* (head) on his way to the chaplain. It serves no useful purpose, as shown by the bored indifference of the guards. ✪ Underline the two phrases that describe this attitude of the guards escorting Alex.

Organizing some thoughts

❓ Fill in the missing word in the following quotations and ask yourself what the quote reveals about a character or a theme in the novel. Learn the quotations by heart; they can be used later in an essay.

> When a man cannot _____ he ceases to be a man.
> Soon we may be needing all our prison space for _____ offenders.
> Is a man who chooses the bad perhaps in some way _____ than a man who has the good imposed upon him?

❓ Go through the three chapters of Part 2 and note in the margin each reference to a violent act. What is the total number and what does this information add to our understanding of the theme of violence in the novel?

❓ Name the character being referred to:
> she breaks into tears when she sees him
> he was killed with an iron bar
> they have a *hopeless sort of a von* (smell)
> he comes to feel there is no trust in the world
> he wants to kill what he calls the criminal reflex
> he speaks of *hard ethical questions* to consider

(Answers on p. 80.)

? Different attitudes towards punishment are expressed in these three chapters. Draw a Mind Map for attitudes towards violence featuring the following characters: prison governor; chaplain; government minister; Alex's fellow prisoners. For each character, think of words that describe aspects of their attitude and add the words to the Mind Map. Make up some icons to represent their ideas.

? Score the following statements 0–5 according to how far you agree with them (0 = completely disagree). Think of examples from the story to support your scoring.

1 The chaplain's strength rests with his point of view; his weakness is that he fails to act on it.

2 Prison has brought about a change in Alex's character.

3 Alex is quite naive and inexperienced at this stage.

Well done my droog (friend)! Time for a break.

Chapter 4

◆ Alex undergoes his first course of treatment.

This chapter makes clear the nature of Ludovico's Technique. Alex is forced to endure scenes of extreme violence while the previously administered drugs work to produce a strong feeling of nausea in him at the events depicted on the screen. Some of the scenes of violence are similar to those which Alex himself used to inflict on innocent victims, but there is no suggestion that Alex realizes this. His reactions to the films are physical, not moral, as he suffers from nausea, aches in his stomach, pains in his head and a strong thirst.

In this chapter there are some understated details that contribute to the growing sense that there are totalitarian aspects to the society that Alex inhabits. When Dr Brodsky makes his appearance, Alex notices how well dressed he is.

❂ Identify this moment in the chapter and try to find an almost identical phrase used to describe someone in Chapter 2 of Part 2. Both Dr Brodsky and the government minister are dressed in the *height of fashion* and the quality of their suits is observed. To some extent this just reflects Alex's keen eye for dress details, but it is also pertinent that the doctor is associated, at least in appearance, with a politician. It suggests the possibility that Dr Brodsky is more than a disinterested doctor, scientifically pursuing a course of treatment, and his motives are rendered suspicious in another way as well. Both the doctor and his colleagues take an unprofessional delight in subjecting Alex to the treatment. The final paragraph of this chapter confirms the reader's view that this is no ordinary clinical trial.

Alex also makes the observation about one of the films he is being shown, one featuring the repeated rape of a woman, that it was convincingly real. It makes him wonder how the film could possibly have been made, given the subject matter. It is possible, of course, that the film had been confiscated by the police without anyone being in a position to have prevented it being made in the first place. Alex's remark also seems to be suggesting the possibility that the authorities didn't care where or how the film was made because all they were interested in was using a film like this for the purposes of applying Ludovico's Technique.

LANGUAGE, STYLE AND STRUCTURE

It was noted in the main 'Language, style and structure' section of this guide that Burgess saw the *nasdat* language as a device by which he could depict scenes of extreme violence without having the reader become too emotionally involved. Burgess spoke of 'protecting' readers when they read the book, as if **explicit** descriptions of violence and sex might engage their *baser instincts*. The author seems to be suggesting that everyone is capable of being aroused by language that explicitly evokes scenes of violence and sex. ❂ Would you agree with this suggestion?

Reread those paragraphs in this chapter where Alex describes the scenes he is forced to watch and underline some of the phrases used to describe violence. ❂ Is it the case that a phrase like *booting his nagoy plott* has a different effect to a phrase of plain English that describes the violence?

It may be the case that it is not just the reader who is being protected by the kind of language used to describe unpleasant acts. ✪ When Alex talks of *the old in-out* as a way of describing a brutal sexual assault, does the language allow him to evade facing up to what exactly is taking place? Is it possible that Alex cannot feel any remorse for his victims because his language acts as a kind of shield, coming between him and an awareness of what he is doing?

Chapter 5

◆ Alex is assured that the treatment is making him better.
◆ Dreaming of violence, Alex finds himself feeling sick.

Despite assurances that he is being made healthy, Alex is perplexed at the way his treatment is developing. Watching the films makes him feel sick and yet he is told this is a good sign. *You are being made sane*, Dr Branom tells him. Alex's confusion about what is happening makes it clear that no one has given him a proper explanation of the nature of the treatment and the principles upon which it is based. In fact, an element of deception is involved – something that was first hinted at in Chapter 4 when Alex asked about the injections he was told he would receive. He naively wonders if they contain vitamins and Dr Branom answers with a reassuring smile, *Something like that*. The reader now knows this to be a calculated act of deception.

Alex is not only a guinea pig for a politically motivated medical experiment, but he is being kept in the dark about what is happening to him. His free will is not seen as necessary. The reason for this lack of concern over his free will soon becomes obvious because the whole point of the treatment is that it eliminates his free will.

Alex is not yet aware of what is happening to his free will as regards violence, but he gets an inkling when the Discharge Officer sarcastically invites him to throw a punch: *But it was funny that starry chelloveck asking for a tolchock in the litso. And it was funny feeling sick like that*. His dream that night confirms the strange new association that is developing between thoughts of violence and feelings of nausea. Dreams have been used before in the novel to point ahead to significant developments. ✪ Can you recall the dream that Alex had towards the end of Part 1 (look back to Chapter 4 if you are not sure), and the dream that his father experienced (Chapter 5)?

Alex is young and inexperienced, but he is beginning to sense something sinister about the situation he is in. After waking from his disturbing dream and wanting to visit the washroom because of his feeling of nausea, Alex discovers that his bedroom door is locked. For the first time he also notices that the window has bars. Alex is still in prison, notwithstanding the polite manners of those about him. What has probably contributed to Alex's naivety about his present situation is the lack of institutional violence. Dr Brodsky and his associates are not like the *tolchocking* wardens he is used to. ✪ However, going back to the point about Alex being deliberately deceived as to the kind of treatment he is receiving, is it possible to describe what has been done to Alex as also an act of violence? Like a prisoner facing a state execution by electrocution, he has been strapped into a chair. Unlike the condemned prisoner, Alex is not fully aware of what is happening and does not realize the effect of the injections and the films of violence.

In Chapter 3 of Part 2, the chaplain tried to excuse his own moral cowardice by thinking that at least Alex chose to be deprived of his ethical will. *So I shall like to think*, he adds, as if knowing really that this is not the case. After reading Chapter 5, the reader knows that the chaplain had good reason for doubting his own line of reasoning.

Chapter 6

◆ Alex is angry when he hears Beethoven's music as part of his treatment.
◆ Dr Brodsky explains the principle behind his treatment.

By accident, the music of Beethoven forms the soundtrack for a film of Nazi atrocities shown to Alex. The full implications of this will not become obvious until later in the story, but at this stage Alex knows enough about his situation to feel very angry about what is happening. In contrast with Alex, Dr Brodsky is completely ignorant about music and can only appreciate it in very philistine terms as *a useful emotional heightener.* Anthony Burgess shares a little joke with the reader by labelling the treatment the Ludovico Technique – Ludwig van being the first part of Beethoven's name.

Dr Brodsky is willing to explain the nature of the treatment because now it is too late for Alex to change his mind. The totalitarian nature of the doctor's approach is hinted at in phrases such as *You can't get the better of us,* and Alex tests the system by one day trying to reject the nurse's injection. The response is a violent one, with Alex held down by force by a group of assistants and assaulted in the process. This is another instance of the pervasive institutional violence that characterizes Alex's society. There is also no doubt that the course of treatment is extremely hard for Alex to endure. One morning he tries to knock himself unconscious in a fruitless endeavour to escape the ordeal. At this stage, the treatment is beginning to work because Alex's self-inflicted violence produces the conditioned response and makes him unable to continue with his plan.

This chapter draws to a close with convincing evidence that Alex has indeed been cured of his violent tendencies. One morning, without being given the usual injection, he finds himself crying at a film of the Holocaust. Alex makes sense of what is happening by talking of the treatment as like a vaccination *cruising about in my krovvy* (blood) and always making him sick when confronted with any image or thought of violence. The treatment may be effective from a practical point of view but not from an ethical one. ❷ Is Alex crying at the Holocaust because he feels the horror of what happened to the Jews under Nazism?

Conclusive evidence of the success of the treatment comes at the end of the chapter with his failed attempt to escape. Once again Alex receives the obligatory beating, *a fair old tolchock clean on the litso,* from the assistant for having disturbed his evening. Violence is very much taken for granted in the society of *A Clockwork Orange* and the young Alex's liking for violence is beginning to seem less and less unusual. ❂ Can you see Alex as in some sense a victim of a violent society? The author, however, is not portraying Alex in a simplistic manner as the helpless victim of a violent age. The sheer nastiness of his violent behaviour was not evaded in Part 1 and his attempt to hoodwink the doctor into thinking he is cured shows how cynical Alex can be. All the same though, Alex is a spirited young man who has grown up in a depressed environment where violence is taken for granted. He entered into violent situations out of his own free will. Now he will try to avoid all such violent situations, but this time it will not be out of his free will.

Dr Brodsky speaks the language of science, not art, and in this chapter he tells Alex the principle behind his treatment – *association, the oldest educational method in the world.* The injections induce nausea and revulsion in a way that is associated with acts of violence, and the intense nature of the treatment acts as an effective form of brainwashing.

It's a sin cries Alex when he realizes the music of Beethoven is being used in a context of violence. The use of a theological term like 'sin' in this situation, especially when uttered by a teenage criminal, carries with it a degree of dramatic surprise. Even the two doctors seem mildly interested by the concept. One might have expected the chaplain to introduce the term but instead the word is spoken by Alex. After all, it is Alex who is experiencing the sense of an outrage being committed. It is because he genuinely loves and appreciates the music of Beethoven that he reacts so passionately to its being used in this way. His use of the word 'sin' also expresses his outrage at the violation of his free will.

The idea that Ludovico's Technique is an assault on the essence of man's ethical nature – choosing to be good is only meaningful when there is the freedom to choose to be bad – is not expressed here in criminal, political or psychological terms. It is not seen as a crime against an individual, or as a totalitarian method of social control, or as an exercise in brainwashing. It is all of these things but in this passage it is spoken of in theological terms, as sin. This exploration of ideas led *Time* Magazine to praise *A Clockwork Orange* as a philosophical novel – adding that such novels are a rarity in English literature. Showing how this idea is developed in the novel will involve unpacking the philosophy behind the theology.

LANGUAGE, STYLE AND STRUCTURE

Dr Branom (played as a woman in Kubrick's film) provides his colleague Dr Brodsky with a summary of what he knows about *nasdat* language: *most of the roots are Slav. Propaganda. Subliminal penetration.* To understand this explanation, remember that the novel was written at the height of the Cold War between the USA and the USSR. The author is projecting his story only about ten years into the future, so it can be assumed that the Cold War is still going on. Most of the *nasdat* words do have their origin in the Slav language and Dr Branom indicates that they have entered the language as part of a propaganda war between the two superpowers. He identifies the process as one of *subliminal penetration.* Burgess, in his autobiography, says how he enjoyed the irony of having teenagers speak like this for 'there was a fine irony in the notion of a teenage race, untouched by politics, using totalitarian brutality as an end in itself, equipped with a dialect which drew on the two chief political languages of the age'.

Chapter 7

◆ Alex is forced to demonstrate that he has been cured of violent tendencies.

◆ The chaplain tries to protest but to no avail.

The official ceremony that demonstrates Alex's changed behaviour is the conclusion to events that began at the end of Chapter 2 in Part 2. It was there that the minister visited the prison as the first part of his government's resolve to tackle the problem of crime with a completely new method of treatment. The aim, he stated, was to *kill the criminal reflex.* Alex's enforced performance indicates that this has been achieved.

The selected audience are there to witness the effectiveness of Ludovico's Technique and most of them are suitably impressed by the show. Alex is not only incapable of being violent but he is, as Dr Brodsky puts it, *impelled towards the good* in his anxiety to avoid the physical distress that is part of the conditioned response. The first demonstration shows Alex being confronted by an aggressive individual who attacks Alex for no stated reason. ✪ Does this kind of attack remind you of a scene from earlier in the story? You may be thinking of Alex's attack on a man near a library in the opening chapter of the book. Dr Brodsky and the government are both pleased with the result of the demonstration, graphic evidence of the change in Alex. Their aim is to reduce the crime rate and relieve the overcrowding in prisons. The new Alex is one less prison inmate, and one less potential violent offender.

Earlier in the story, the chaplain was reluctant to take his criticism of the treatment too far. He was worried about going against what was clearly government policy and upsetting the authorities. Now, confronted by the spectacle of Alex's conditioned responses, he feels compelled to speak out. He points out that Alex has no choice in the matter and only acts the way he does because he is driven by fear of physical pain. No moral decision is made because there is no act of free will. The absence of free will, argues the chaplain, does cure him of wrongdoing but also robs him of moral choice. Alex adds to the debate by reminding the audience that he has lost some vital part of being human. *Am I just to be like a clockwork orange?* he asks. ✪ Remind yourself where this phrase was first heard in the story.

Alex's question about being reduced to a clockwork orange is dealt with by a supporter of the treatment. He tells Alex that he made the choice and he is now bearing the consequences. ✪ What choice is the speaker referring to? The speaker could have in mind the written agreement that Alex signed in the prison governor's office in Chapter 3. If so, then there is some doubt about the degree of choice because Alex was not at that time aware of the nature of the treatment to which he was submitting. The speaker could also be referring to the more general idea that Alex chose a life of violence and crime in the first place.

✪ How do you feel about Alex after seeing the demonstrations of his changed behaviour? The chaplain describes what has

been seen as a *grotesque act of self-abasement,*
'abasement' meaning 'humiliation' and 'degradation'
whether you agree with the chaplain's opinion. Look
especially at the scene where Alex desperately tries to appease
the man who has just refused to accept his razor weapon as a
token of submission. Alex gets down on his knees and kisses
his boots, and there is certainly something pathetic and
humiliating about this behaviour.

Dr Brodsky exclaims that Alex will now be the *true Christian*
and that he will turn the other cheek rather than inflict
violence. The notion of turning the other cheek, a Christian
concept found in the New Testament, is mentioned earlier, at
the end of the previous chapter. Dr Brodsky is wrong because
the Christian concept is fundamentally tied in with free will.
The true Christian chooses to turn the other cheek when one
side of his face has already been hit. The Christian willingly
rejects violence by presenting the other cheek, preferring this
to be also hit rather than retaliate with a show of violence.
This is not the motivation behind Alex's conduct.

His gallant behaviour towards the sexy woman who is brought
before him is equally unmotivated by any moral concern.
Quite the opposite, in fact, because when he first sees the
woman his first thoughts are lecherous and violent ones. It is
his desperate desire to avoid feeling painfully sick that
motivates him to drop to his knees and play the role of the
honourable knight. This is what Dr Brodsky meant when he
said that Alex is *impelled towards the good by, paradoxically,
being impelled towards evil.* It is interesting that Alex notices
the reactions of other people in the audience towards the sexy
woman, fuelled by *dirty and unholy desire.* ❂ Why do you
think the author has Alex make this observation of people in
the audience?

Time to take stock

❔ The following list covers eight key moments in Part 2
but they are in alphabetical order, not the order in
which they occur. Try re-ordering them without
looking at the novel. Then check your answer. Make

corrections, so that you end up with a
...rrect order.

...onstration shows Alex to be cured of violent
...ncies.

...x is sentenced to 14 years in prison.

...hurch music is Alex's only comfort in prison.

...Nominated as a suitable case for treatment, Alex
starts watching films.

Objections to the Ludovico Technique are
expressed to Alex by the chaplain.

Sorrow is felt by the chaplain over the success of
the treatment.

Totalitarian methods are used to administer the
treatment to Alex.

When Alex's cell becomes badly overcrowded, a
new prisoner is beaten to death.

A possible mnemonic for the correct sequence could
be: **A** **c**lockwork **o**range **w**ill **n**ot **t**aste **as** **s**weet.

? Draw a Mind Map with Alex in the centre and place
round him the characters of Dr Brodsky, the
government minister, the chaplain and the prison
governor. Summarize each character's attitude
towards Alex. Add another branch for Alex's attitude
towards his own situation at the end of Chapter 7.

? The government minister would probably agree with
all of the following statements. Which one best sums
up his position in Part 2 of the novel?

the cost of running prisons must be reduced
traditional punishments are not working
the end justifies the means
reducing the crime rate and making the streets
safe

(Answer on p. 80)

Now relax and enjoy a cup of chai (tea).

P*art 3*

Chapter 1

♦ Alex is released from prison and he returns home.
♦ His bedroom has been rented to a lodger and his parents are not expecting him.
♦ Alex leaves and tells his parents they will not see him again.

The opening of this chapter makes clear the political context of Ludovico's Technique and its relation to the issue of crime and punishment. A general election is only weeks away and the government is pinning its hopes of re-election on its success in reducing the crime rate. Alex reads in a pro-government newspaper that the pay of police officers has been increased and that sterner methods are being taken against criminals. His own treatment is part of all this, as the story on page two of the newspaper indicates. There is also some evidence to suggest that the new measures are having some effect because the vandalism in his apartment block has gone.

Alex also learns that he is the first *graduate* of the State Institute for Reclamation of Criminal Types, and that the government minister is promising a new era of crime-free living. The previous chapter raised ethical questions about the value and effect of Ludovico's Technique and this chapter reinforces them by pointing to the political motivation of those organizing this response to the problem of violent crime. The government wants to reduce crime because doing so will help it to get re-elected and not because it is genuinely concerned. The government has embraced Ludovico's Technique, despite the serious ethical issues it raises, because the method promises concrete results. ✪ What do you think is the right way to approach the problem of crime and violence in our society?

The title of the treatment centre, the State Institute for Reclamation of Criminal Types, is revealing because of the word *types*. This would seem to indicate that criminals like Alex are seen as belonging to a certain type rather than as individuals. This fits in with the scientific nature of the course of treatment because Dr Brodsky has developed a technique that will presumably work on the mind or brain of any violent criminal. Dr Brodsky is not working to understand why a particular person becomes a criminal; he is merely concerned with changing behaviour through conditioning. It is part of the novel's dystopian vision of society that this solution is adopted, rather than dealing with the social causes.

Alex has been thrown into a very adult world for the past two years of his life. It is easy for the reader to forget that when he is released he is still only seventeen years old. There are poignant reminders of his youthfulness, beginning with him looking forward to returning home after he leaves the café: *a nice surprise for dadada and mum … then I could lay back on my own malenky bed and slooshy some lovely music.* Suddenly there is a glimpse of Alex as a teenage boy relishing the prospect of getting back to his home and his own bedroom. ✪ If you have read the novel, can you identify the **irony** in this quotation? If you have not yet read the whole story you might have a doubt anyway about Alex being able to enjoy his music.

The most poignant reminder that Alex is not an adult comes towards the end of the chapter when he has to acknowledge the fact that he no longer has a bedroom to call his own and that his weak-minded parents seem unable to offer him assistance. Alex may be a hardened young criminal, one responsible for the death of one of his victims, but when he senses that his parents don't care he breaks down and cries. It is left to the lodger, Joe, to point out that Alex is paying for his crimes. When Alex feels sorry for himself, *Nobody wants or loves me. I've suffered and suffered …*, Joe reminds him that he has made innocent people suffer: *it's only right you should suffer proper.* There is, of course, some truth in this, and if Alex were an adult it might be difficult to feel sorry for him. ✪ How do you feel about Alex at this stage? Is he getting his just deserts or is he in some sense a victim of society?

It is possible that Alex's tearful response to his situation is related to the effects of his conditioning because he is no longer the same person who began the treatment two weeks earlier. This comes out in the scene in which his father explains how Alex's property has been confiscated for the purpose of compensating the victims of his crime. ✪ Can you identify the sentence that registers a physical response in Alex related to his treatment? Alex's headache and his raging thirst suggest that his reaction to his father's information would have been a violent one. He is unable to react in this way and has to deal with the situation some other way. The way in which his emotional responses have been affected by his conditioning becomes clearer in the next chapter, but this incident is an indication that all is not right with Alex.

Try this

? At this stage, you ought to have a *nasdat* dictionary that is fairly complete (approaching 200 words if you have noted every one). Here are some words that appear in this chapter. Check that your meanings for them are correct (answers on p. 81). Then add them to your dictionary.

> *cutter, kupetted, jeezny, rabbit, knopka, minootas, sharries*

Chapter 2

- ◆ Alex discovers he can no longer listen to his favourite music.
- ◆ He returns to the milkbar and feels suicidal after taking a drug.
- ◆ Attacked in the library by a man he once assaulted, Alex is rescued by the police.

The full effects of Ludovico's Technique become plain in this chapter. The treatment seems to have worked in that any thought of violence produces an instant physiological reaction. The clearest demonstration of this occurs in the library scene when Alex is set upon by the senior citizen who had previously been one of his victims. Alex's inability to resist the group attack led by the senior citizen results, almost comically, in the spectacle of him welcoming the attendant's intention to call the police. Alex himself is reduced to a state where he felt *I could just flick at them and they would all fall over, but I just let myself be held very patient.* ❷ Read the account of this scene in the library again and write down a word that conveys your attitude towards Alex at this stage.

Some readers may feel, remembering the treatment of the senior citizen in the book's opening chapter, that Alex is receiving what he deserves. In the way that the author describes the scene in the library, however, there is something pitiable about Alex's predicament. If Alex were acting from his free will then the quotation above would suggest a Christ-like act of forgiveness on his part. It is his complete lack of free will that renders him pathetic. The scene in which he is set upon by a group of geriatrics becomes almost laughable.

Ludovico's Technique has changed Alex in more than one way. He is not just incapable of acting violently, his whole nature seems to have undergone a change. In the opening scene in the music store, Alex is mocked for his choice of Mozart, but he has to be careful because he feels himself growing *all razdraz within* at the mockery. He knows what the physiological response will be and so he smiles at those belittling him. The word *razdraz* (upset) was used in Part 1, Chapter 3, when Pete annoyed Alex by criticizing his treatment of Dim. Before his treatment, when Alex felt upset he used to deal with it by violence, so perhaps the treatment is so finely tuned that even a feeling of distress is enough to trigger off the conditioned response.

Evidence that the effect goes further than this, that his whole set of emotional responses has been altered, comes when he goes into the booth to listen to some of his favourite music. As far as we know, Mozart was not played during his course of treatment but *any music that was like for the emotions would make me sick*. Another unintended effect of the treatment occurs in the library when Alex consults a medical book. Pictures of injuries and wounds trigger off the conditioned response, as does the Bible and its tales involving violence.

Alex enters a severe state of depression. This is partly a reaction to his overall situation at being rejected by his parents, losing his bedroom, discovering he cannot even enjoy the music that was the one sustaining love of his life and generally feeling that he is no longer in control of himself. It may also be related to his course of treatment in that the intense conditioning has altered his set of emotional responses. In many respects, the Alex who emerges from prison after his treatment is not the same person of two weeks earlier.

The scene in the milkbar has Alex contemplating suicide. It begins with his choice of a drug, the effects of which were first noted in the first chapter of the book. ✪ Can you recall how Alex described the effects of this drug? (Look back to the start of Chapter 1 to confirm what was said there.) He had called it a *cowardly* drug because of the way it sapped the will, yet now it becomes his choice of escape from the pressures around him. He starts speaking the kind of nonsense that was first heard coming from the sad character in Chapter 1, indicating Alex's decline. In losing his free will, Alex has also lost the will to live. This becomes apparent in his hallucinogenic daydream where he experiences a terrible sense of loss and emptiness. Dreams, even drug-induced ones, are used to pinpoint significant moments in the novel and the dream here marks the depth of despair into which Alex has sunk.

The attack on Alex in the library is rich in irony. Nonetheless the behaviour of the elderly citizens reveals yet another way in which violence permeates the society. Their level of violence may be laughably weak – although Alex feels a punch delivered right on the nose – but the vehemence of their violent inclinations is not: *Kill him, stamp on him, murder him, kick his teeth in*. It may be, as Alex observes, *old age having a go at youth*, but it is also symptomatic of the dystopian society of *A Clockwork Orange* that so many sections of the community resort to violence.

The attack in the library is undertaken in a spirit of retribution, an attitude the senior citizens share with the prison governor. ✪ Can you remember the governor's attitude towards crime and punishment? One of the elderly readers in the library takes this attitude to an extreme and calls for criminals like Alex to be *exterminated ... like so many noisome pests*. ✪ Can you see a way in which the government has adopted a similar kind of attitude, though not literally?

LANGUAGE, STYLE AND STRUCTURE

It was noted in the main 'Language, style and structure' section of this guide, under 'Structure', that certain settings first seen in Part 1 recur in Part 3. In Chapter 1 of this final part we saw Alex returning home; in Chapter 2 he revisits the music shop and the milkbar, and he encounters once again the man who frequents the library. These places and people, all first featured in the novel's early chapters, now register with Alex in a changed way. Time has passed, circumstances have changed and so also has Alex. The structure of the novel encapsulates these changes by having the early chapters of Part 3 refer back to places and moments from the early chapters of Part 1. As you read the next two chapters, look for more structural similarities.

Beware of confusing the book and the film when referring to the attack on Alex in the library. The encounter with the man coming home from the library in Chapter 1 does not feature in the film so there cannot be a recognition scene involving him later on. In the interest of economy, presumably, Kubrick left out this scene because in one sense it is similar to the attack on the drunk in Chapter 2, which is in the film. The recognition scene in the film involves the drunk man instead. His associates are a gathering of down-and-outs under a nearby bridge. These characters serve the same purpose as the mob of elderly people in the library.

Chapter 3

◆ Alex's rescuers turn out to include Dim and Billyboy.
◆ Alex is driven into the countryside and beaten up by the police.

Violence has been seen to be a part of the culture of both the police and the prison authorities, so the opening paragraph of this chapter, describing how the police enjoy using violence to disperse Alex's attackers, does not come as a great surprise. Indeed, so common is violence in the society of *A Clockwork Orange* that this additional but minor instance of it can pass by almost unnoticed. The rest of the chapter, however, does not allow the reader to lose sight of this characteristic feature of the novel's society. It is interesting that the account of the police beating inflicted on Alex does not dwell on Alex's conditioned response to violence. To judge from the demonstration presented in Chapter 7 of Part 2, Alex presumably begs for forgiveness and tries to lick the boots of his assailants. ✪ Why do you think the author does not refer to this in the description of Alex's beating?

One answer to this question is that the author has already covered the way in which Alex now responds to violence and that here he is concerned with a different aspect of violence. The strongest impression that comes across in the description of Alex's beating is the casualness and predictability of it. *Just a malenky bit of summary*, says Dim. The chapter's penultimate paragraph conveys the casualness of what follows, through its description of the police car driver. The driver's indifference to what takes place – presumably he has seen it many times before – indicates the degree to which violence has become institutionalized in the police force. Note that in Kubrick's film this aspect is not emphasized to the same degree in this scene because there is no car driver. The punishment of Alex is presented instead as a personal act of revenge, whereas in the book the utter casualness of such a beating is what is emphasized.

This scene in the book can be put alongside other examples of how violence is taken for granted in teenage gang culture, in prisons, and even amongst senior citizens. In this context Alex's violence becomes more understandable. He expresses himself through violence, just as Dim and Billyboy do as gang members, and as they continue to do as part of their adult police culture. It is this general culture of violence that helps explain how the government adopts its own violent assault on people's individuality by way of Ludovico's Technique. In this way, the overall acceptance of violence is part of the theme of dystopia that runs through the novel.

The violence administered to Alex makes up *the old summary*, Billyboy's term for his police force's use of summary punishment. The police, putting into direct practice the attitude of the prison governor (as seen at the beginning of Chapter 3 of Part 2), have taken upon themselves the task of administering punishment for crimes committed.

There is irony in having the violent punishment carried out by Dim and Billyboy. They were deadly rivals in their youth, even though they shared an opposition to the police, and yet here they are together and representing the force of law and order. From Dim's point of view, they have simply grown up: *That's what we was, young droogie. And you it was that was always the youngest. And here now we are.*

In the first chapter of Part 2, Alex learns that Georgie has died as the result of a botched break-in and robbery. In Kubrick's film, however, he becomes Dim's fellow police officer instead of Billyboy. This does not go against the spirit of the book because it is as understandable for someone like Georgie to become a policeman as it is for Dim. However, be sure to refer to the book version, not the film, in your essays.

The encounter between Alex, Dim and Billyboy takes the reader back to an earlier encounter involving these three characters. ✪ Look back to Part 1, Chapter 2, and identify the similarities and differences between the two scenes. It is worth making the point here that in order to impress an examiner you would also need to show the significance of these similarities and differences. For example, the two incidents show the way in which violence is casually accepted by groups within society. Violence is not just an aspect of street gangs, it is woven more deeply into society and both Dim and Billyboy are able to progress from being hooligans to police officers with apparent ease.

Before your break, spend a few minootas (minutes) on this

❓ Find a quotation from Chapters 1–3 to support each of these statements. See if your teacher agrees with you.

The government hopes to get re-elected on the success of its anti-crime programme.
Alex can no longer enjoy his favourite music.
The use of violence is taken for granted by the police.

❓ Try this quiz on Chapters 1–3. (Answers on p. 81.)

What is the name of the new institution created by the government to administer Ludovico's Technique?
Who does Alex resemble when he re-visits the milkbar?
Who carries a whip?
Why do the police prefer to beat people up in the countryside?

? In the chart below, tick which statements apply to the book and which apply to the film.
(Answers on p. 81.)

event	book	film
• Alex starts to grow up		
• Alex keeps a pet snake		
• Dr Branom is a man		
• Alex is recognized by a drunk he had earlier attacked		
• Georgie dies at the hands of someone he attacked		

Chapter 4

◆ Alex turns up at the home of the man he had once attacked.
◆ The man befriends Alex and listens to his account of what has happened.

The man who befriends Alex, the author of a text called *A Clockwork Orange*, expresses the same attitude towards Ludovico's Technique as the prison chaplain. When he says *a man who cannot choose ceases to be a man*, the words could have been spoken by the chaplain. Both men share the same fundamental objection to the conditioning but, unlike the chaplain, this man wants to use the abuse of Alex for a political cause.

The crudeness of Ludovico's Technique becomes clearer in this chapter. In the previous chapter, when Alex tried listening to some Mozart, it was seen how he could no longer enjoy classical music. Now, we learn, *music and the sexual act, literature and art* are all affected by the nature of the treatment.

LANGUAGE, STYLE AND STRUCTURE

The return of Alex to the house that he attacked in Chapter 2 of Part 1 is the most dramatic of the structural similarities between the early and late parts of the novel. Details of the two scenes reinforce one another so that the irony is inescapable. In the first visit to the house, for instance, the false story that Alex used to gain entry now becomes a true version of what has taken place. The man, who at the earlier time was in the process of writing about the notion of a clockwork orange, is now confronted with a very real example. When the man says, at the very end of the chapter, that both his wife and Alex are victims of the age there is some truth in this. His wife became a victim of a nasty gang of youths and Alex has become a victim to what might be called a nasty gang of politicians.

Chapter 5

- ◆ F. Alexander begins to link Alex with the earlier attack on his home.
- ◆ Associates of F. Alexander take Alex to an apartment and leave him there.
- ◆ Alex, unable to escape the sound of classical music, is driven to attempt suicide.

The man who befriends Alex, now identified as F. Alexander, seems to be motivated by a mixture of politics and religion. In his book *A Clockwork Orange*, F. Alexander strikes Alex as perhaps a little *bezoomny* (crazy) and he does act a little strangely. He talks of ordinary people needing to be *prodded* into an awareness of this threat to freedom and accompanies this remark with the stabbing of a kitchen fork into the wall. He also tells Alex that the government's policy is the beginning of a descent into totalitarianism. He raises the question of whether the government might use Ludovico's Technique to *pump out the life and guts and will of whoever sees fit to displease the Government*. This is not altogether fantasy on his part because the reader recalls the visit of the government minister to the Staja in Part 2, Chapter 2, and his remark there that prisons would soon be needed for political prisoners.

Although F. Alexander does not seem to belong to any particular political party, he does want to use Alex to attack the government. It is apparent that one of his associates, Rubinstein, has a closer link with an opposition party, because he promises Alex that *the Party will not be ungrateful* for Alex's assistance in exposing the government to criticism. Alex is right to start wondering if any of them have any interest in Alex as a person who is suffering. When he exclaims *stop treating me like a thing that's got to be just used*, Alex is unwittingly drawing a comparison between the government politicians and the likes of opposition politicians like Rubinstein. In their own ways they are both exploiting Alex and it is part of the dystopian nature of the novel's world that the political system is seen in this way.

More alarming for your *humble narrator* at this stage is F. Alexander's growing awareness that Alex was the young hooligan who broke into his house. Alex is keen to leave the house and does not question being placed in an apartment on his own. The loud playing of classical music does not seem to be a coincidence, and it drives Alex to attempt suicide.
✪ Can you think of two possible explanations for the deliberate playing of music that Alex cannot tolerate?

Chapter 6

◆ Alex recovers in hospital and finds himself cured.
◆ He is visited by the government minister who praises his recovery.
◆ Alex looks forward to returning to his old ways.

Alex dimly recalls being visited in hospital by the prison chaplain, a man who has left his job because he can no longer reconcile himself to the kind of treatment that Alex has received. He is also visited by the three associates of F. Alexander whom Alex has good reason to suspect. Alex's recovery from the effects of the conditioning is first brought to our attention through a characteristic device of the author, the recalled dream. ✪ Briefly remind yourself of other moments in the story where a recalled dream pointed ahead to a development in the story.

Earlier in the novel, Alex was being 'cured' of the violence that was a part of his personality. Ironically the 'cure' became the new 'disease', and he is now cured of this in the sense that Ludovico's Technique no longer controls his responses to certain ideas and situations; violence no longer repels him. When he dreams of running people down in a stolen car and raping women, he suffers none of the painful associations that Ludovico's Technique previously conditioned in him. This is a **paradox** because the evidence that Alex has recovered his free will consists of him freely choosing to inflict pain and suffering on others. It is as if the author wants to say to you, as the reader, that you can't have it both ways. Violent behaviour can be eliminated but only if you accept people being reduced to a zombie-like state of conditioned responses. If, on the other hand, you want people to have free will then it has to be accepted that they may exercise it in some very unpleasant ways.

Further evidence of Alex's full recovery comes in the scene in which his parents visit him. Their lodger Joe has left suddenly, having becoming involved in an incident with the police. Alex enjoys the irony of what has led to his bedroom becoming once more available. What Alex enjoys most, though, is the feeling that he is once more his old self, in control of his situation and able to boss his parents about in a way that is familiar to him. He senses the paradox himself when he says: *It was like as though to get better I had had to get worse.*

The visit of the Minister of the Interior clears up uncertainty in the mind of the reader over what exactly led to Alex trying to kill himself. What emerges is that F. Alexander was deliberately informed by his associates about the identity of Alex in the expectation that this would drive the writer to seek revenge. They fully hoped to be able to use Alex's suicide as political ammunition against the government. Alex did not die, however, and the government has discovered the plot against them and put F. Alexander in prison. This opens the way for the government to make political capital by restoring Alex to his old self and gaining credit for doing so.

○ Has Alex grown up and learnt from his experiences? On the face of it, there is little evidence to suggest he has. His dreams of violence and his treatment of his parents suggest he has simply returned to his old ways. At the end of the chapter someone presents him with something to sign and he does so without thinking, *not knowing what I was signing and not, O my brothers, caring either.* ❸ Why do you think Alex is asked to sign some papers before he is released from hospital? The important point is that Alex signs the paper in the same casual manner that he signed the papers giving the government permission to condition him in the first place.

 ### LANGUAGE, STYLE AND STRUCTURE

The American edition of *A Clockwork Orange* ends with this chapter, as does the film version directed by Stanley Kubrick. In his autobiography, Burgess explains how the film ended and how he felt about it:

> Alex, the thug-hero, having been conditioned to hate violence, is now deconditioned and sees himself wrestling with a naked girl while a crowd dressed for Ascot discreetly applauds. Alex's voice-over gloats: 'I was cured all right.' A vindication of free will had become an exaltation of the urge to sin. I was worried.

What worries Anthony Burgess is that the film, following the American edition of the book, concludes with the paradox that was noted above. The last chapter of the book, showing how Burgess brought *his* story to a conclusion, helps explain his dismay at the ending shown in the film and in American editions of the book.

Chapter 7

◆ Alex has a new gang but feels dissatisfied.

Alex has returned to familiar territory, sitting in the milkbar with his new gang members and wondering what to do with the evening ahead. Alex has taken his favourite drugged drink, *the old moloko with knives in it*, and as before he likes to describe his personal appearance. Although Dim, Pete and Georgie have been replaced by Len, Rick and Bully, there is the same kind of tension within the gang arising from the issue of leadership. Alex is once again the acknowledged leader but, as before, he is aware of the insecurity of his role and the fact that Bully would take over if there were a suitable opportunity. ❂ What do you think the author might be saying about youth by re-creating the milkbar scene but with a different set of characters and customers, apart from Alex? One small difference, a change in dress fashion, is quite superficial when put alongside the general sameness of the youth scene over a period of more than two years. The author wants to stress the idea that a youth culture of some kind will always exist and, although some minor differences will change over time, the similarities are more important than the differences. ❂ What would be an equivalent of the milkbar for today's youth culture? How many similarities are there with the youth of the Korova Milkbar?

The important difference between the scene in the milkbar here and the book's opening chapter lies in the attitude of Alex. The change can be appreciated by looking at his attitude towards violence. At first, it looks as though little has changed because, once again, Alex characteristically delivers a blow to a drugged young *chelloveck* sitting beside him before leaving the milkbar. This conscious echo of the first chapter of the novel is taken a stage further when, out on the street, the gang pick on a hapless pedestrian to assault. The difference this time is that Alex is happy to let Bully take the lead in attacking the man, whereas in the first chapter Alex initiated the violence. Alex notes that his willingness to become a mere spectator to violence is becoming increasingly common, as if the prospect of some *ultra-violence* no longer has the same appeal for him. This is confirmed in the scene in the pub when he criticizes his gang members for cowardly attacking defenceless people.

When he leaves the pub, Alex notes the police cars cruising by, and youths on street corners. He reflects on the likelihood that some kind of violence is taking place, yet it fails to arouse his interest. Indeed, he is able to step back from it and observe it as a sociological phenomenon, *it had become like a fight between naughty nadsats and the rozzes.*

The first indication that Alex is not the same young hooligan whom we first encountered in the milkbar comes when he admits that he feels *very bored and a bit hopeless.* In the past, boredom was relieved by violence but now he is content to let Bully do this kind of thing. In the Duke of New York pub, another change is noted when Alex is disinclined to spend his money on drinks for the senior citizens. Now that Alex is working, in the music business and quite legitimately, it is his own hard-earned money in his pocket that he is reluctant to squander. Rick does point out that it is easy to simply steal money but Alex makes no response to this, only noting that his *zoobies* (teeth) are in a poor state. This aspect of Alex's character has not changed: he remains highly sensitive to matters of personal hygiene and appearance.

The fact that Alex keeps a photograph of a baby comes as a surprise to the reader. Although he quickly tears it up, the change in his attitude is confirmed when he accuses his *droogs* of being like children themselves. When Alex leaves his gang to themselves and walks away from the pub on his *oddy knocky* (solitary) he is, in effect, saying goodbye to them and the way of life he had shared with them.

The change in Alex is also reflected in his changing musical tastes. Peaceful songs accompanied by a piano now appeal to him more than the *bolshy orchestras*. Even more surprising, to himself as much as for the reader, he begins to picture himself as growing old and sitting by the fire, grey-haired.

Matters of age come into his conversation with Pete. Aged fifteen when the story began, Alex is now eighteen. *As old as that*, comments Pete who is himself nearly twenty, married and settled into a very peaceful and mundane way of life. The encounter with Pete is momentous because it clarifies in Alex's own mind what is happening: *Oh my brothers. I was like growing up*. In this way, Pete's situation plays an important role in leading Alex to the concluding thoughts that bring the novel to an end. ✪ What is the significance of the fact that Pete, as well as Alex, grows up in this story? Alex is the central character in the novel but the author wants to show that growing up and changing is not something peculiar to him: it is part of life.

The novel draws to an end with Alex's reflections on the nature of youth. He introduces the simile of a mechanical, wind-up toy with a spring that can be wound up and then released. The coiled spring of the toy represents the pent-up energy of youth, waiting to find expression. The reckless motion of the released toy as it *itties* (goes) off *and bangs straight into things bang bang* is like the directionless energy of youth seeking an outlet for its energy. ❍ What is the difference between this simile for youth and the image of a clockwork orange? Both images feature a mechanical toy, but the crucial difference is that young people grow up and in doing so no longer resemble the manic motion of a wound-up toy. Growing up involves orientation, so there is a direction. Pete is directing himself to a happy life with Georgina and occasional word games parties with friends, while Alex is beginning to orientate himself towards the idea of acquiring a girlfriend. The image of a clockwork orange, on the other hand, represents an attempt to arrest a youth's nature and control it by interfering with its natural development.

The novel does not have a simplistic happy ending. Alex concludes that life goes on in *a terrible grahzny vonny world* and with *your old droog Alex all on his oddy knocky seeking like a mate*. This is hardly a 'happy ever after' ending. There is also the realization that even if he does find a mate and have children, they also will have to grow up and pass through the same stages as Alex did. Alex can imagine himself as a father telling all this to his son, but he knows the son will not listen, just as his son's son won't listen to his father either. *And so it would itty on to like the end of the world, round and round and round.* There is a clear sense here of life as a cycle of growing up and passing through adolescence and youth, doomed to be repeated from one generation to the next.

LANGUAGE, STYLE AND STRUCTURE

This chapter consciously echoes the novel's opening chapter, returning the reader to the narrative voice of Alex as he sits in the milkbar one evening and introduces his three *droogs*. ❍ Look back at the first six paragraphs of Chapter 1 in Part 1 and note the similarities in content and language with the opening paragraphs of this chapter.

If you are writing about the structure of *A Clockwork Orange*, make sure that you relate the novel's structure to its meaning. A good example of this connection may be found in this last chapter. The significance of the chapter is that Alex is no longer a disaffected youth seeking an outlet in drugs and violence. This chapter, signalling the fact that he has grown up, is the last Chapter 7. It is the twenty-first chapter, twenty-one being the traditional age of reaching adulthood, and represents the last stage of Alex's development from youth to maturity. In this way, then, describing the structure helps to show how it is related to the author's concerns as expressed in the theme of growing up.

Time to take stock

? Try this exercise with a friend. Taking turns, speak on the topics below for one minute without repeating any words and trying not to hesitate.

Alex's home life and his parents
events leading up to Alex's arrest
role of the chaplain in the novel
principles behind Ludovico's Technique
Alex at the end of the novel

? Record how you feel towards Alex at different points in the story by filling in the chart below.

Scene	My feelings
• Part 1, Ch. 1 Attacks man with library books	
• Part 1, Ch. 2 Attacks woman	
• Part 1, Ch. 6 Alex is arrested	
• Part 2, Ch. 7 Demonstration that Alex is cured	
• Part 3, Ch. 1 Alex returns home from prison	
• Part 3, Ch. 2 Alex attacked in the library	

? How would you film the last chapter of the book? In particular, how would your shots of the opening scene in the milkbar differ from the opening scene of the film in the same location? Also, how would you film the very last moments of the film after Alex has left Pete and Georgina?

? Make up a list of the individuals, groups and institutions that employ violence in the course of the story. For each one, give a page reference that points to a moment in the story that illustrates their violence.

? The following lists sixteen events in Alex's life but not in the right order. Put them in the right order by numbering the statements, so that 1 is the earliest event in the story and 16 the last. (Answers on p. 81)

(a) The government is forced to reverse the treatment on Alex.

(b) A woman is raped and, along with her husband, badly beaten up.

(c) Depressed, Alex goes to the library to find information on suicide.

(d) Non-violent thoughts occupy Alex's mind at the end of the story.

(e) Tensions within the gang lead to a confrontation with Dim and Georgie.

(f) Sent to prison, Alex meets a chaplain and finds out about Ludovico's Technique.

(g) Alex arrives, by coincidence, at the house of people he had earlier attacked.

(h) Alex and his gang attack a man coming from a library.

(i) Alex is set up by his gang and arrested by the police.

(j) Locked in a room, Alex attempts suicide.

(k) Alex is surprised to discover he has grown up.

(l) Attacked in a library, Alex is 'rescued' by the police.

(m) Alex discovers he can no longer enjoy his favourite music.

(n) Dim laughs at someone singing and is hit by Alex for his bad manners.

(**o**) Released from prison, Alex returns home to find his room occupied by a lodger.

(**p**) Alex is selected for treatment and cured of his violent tendencies.

❓ Here is a flowchart for the sixteen events in Alex's life. When you have them in the right order, put them into the appropriate box. The first event is (h) in the list above so (h) goes in the first box. Boxes on the same level indicate events happening around the same time. An arrow indicates that one event has helped cause another.

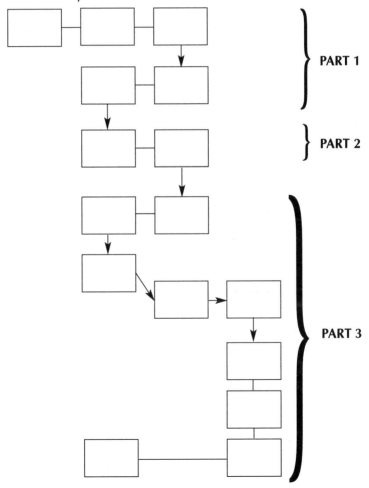

PART 1

PART 2

PART 3

Answers to test sections

PART 1

Now viddy (look at) this (p. 35)

Alex dislikes the way Pete and Georgie are stuffing their mouths with food while beating up the writer in the cottage. At the end of the first paragraph in Chapter 3, Alex comments on Dim's body odour.

girls, mouth, buying, head, sex, girls, eyes, slept

drove, picked up, police, pocket, clothes, playing, smell, little, women, blood, testicles, upset, furious, sleep, underwear, body, key, milk, ripped.

Put your rassoodock (mind) to this (p. 42)

Chapter 4: dream, speaking, wonderful, remarkable. **Chapter 5**: pocket, night, go, money, concern, stupid, voice, one two three. **Chapter 6**: large, houses, valuable, door-bell, on one's own, feet, male and female cats, dirty, bastards, throats. **Chapter 7**: prisoners, sound, horror, loud, stomach, filthy, rich, neck, horrible, noise.

PART 2

Try this (p. 46)

story, words, criminals, breast, old man, mad, police, soiled, Jews, food, led.

Try this (p. 48)

begin, sleep, happened, pillow, guts, kill.

Organizing some thoughts (p. 50)

The missing words are: choose, political, better.

There are at least ten references to violent acts. The number confirms the impression that violence is an everyday aspect of prison life and not something peculiar to just Alex.

The characters referred to are Alex's mother, Georgie, fellow-prisoners, Alex, government minister, the chaplain.

Time to take stock (p. 59)

'The end justifies the means' best sums up his position.

PART 3

Try this (p. 63)

money, bought, life, work, button, minutes, buttocks

Before your break, spend a few minootas (minutes) on this (p. 68)

State Institute for Reclamation of Criminal Types
The drugged character described in Chapter 1 of Part 1
The police
They don't want the public to be aware of what is going on

1 = book, 2 = film, 3= book, 4 = film, 5 = book

Time to take stock (p. 77)

1 = h, 2 = b, 3 = n, 4 = e, 5 = i, 6 = f, 7 = p, 8 = o, 9 = m,
10 = c, 11 = l, 12 = g, 13 = j, 14 = a, 15 = k, 16 = d.

Far more has been written about Kubrick's film *A Clockwork Orange* than about the novel by Anthony Burgess. The reader should be careful to distinguish between the two. Critical comment about the glorification of violence in *A Clockwork Orange* usually refers to the film. However, because the film carries the same title as the book there is room for confusion. One of the most accessible pieces of critical writing on the book may be found in Blake Morrison's introduction to the Penguin edition.

Morrison, in his second paragraph, talks about the powers of the author being 'fully concentrated', and he goes on to list these powers. He mentions the intriguing title, the symmetry of the structure, a central character who both attracts and repels, the dystopian society, the moral dilemma at the heart of the story and, finally, the highly inventive use of language.

In his essay, Morrison says that 'like Milton, Burgess was of the Devil's party without knowing it'. Milton, a seventeenth-century poet, created the character of Satan in his long poem *Paradise Lost.* Most readers agree that he portrayed Satan so sympathetically that he comes across as the most engaging figure in the poem. Similarly, in *A Clockwork Orange*, it is Alex who engages the reader and, as Morrison says, the writing becomes 'most alive when its hero behaves wickedly, not when he is paying for his crimes'. What Morrison is saying here suggests how the reader could develop a very positive approach to Alex, emphasizing his attractive and admirable qualities.

One reason why it is possible to engage positively with Alex is his central role as the narrator, directly addressing the reader and inviting the reader to share his pleasures and woes. Alex's use of language increases his appeal, *Oh, it was gorgeosity and yumyumyum* he tells us when he can once again enjoy the sound of music in the last chapter. *O my brothers* is Alex's way of inviting an alliance between himself and the reader.

This sense of an alliance is strengthened by what we see of his circumstances. His working-class parents struggle to cope with dull jobs in a grim, class-based society. Alex, a passionate individual who seeks to express his sense of selfhood, is left to fend for himself, finding expression in drugs, sex and violence. Indeed, a Marxist critique of the novel might portray Alex very much as a working-class hero struggling against the tyranny and bourgeois values of the State.

Morrison points out that Alex's love of classical music is part of the novel's moral complexity. High art, like the music of Beethoven, can be regarded as one of the characteristics of an advanced culture – an idea which is raised in Part 2, Chapter 4. Alex listens to someone on the radio promoting the arts as a civilizing influence and dismisses the idea with contempt. *Civilised my syphilised yarbles. Music always sort of sharpened me up*, exclaims Alex. Morrison points out that Burgess was well aware of a debate in the early 1960s about the significance of knowing that the men who unleashed the Holocaust were cultivated individuals who read Shakespeare and listened to Beethoven. In the novel, Alex's love of Beethoven and other composers is an authentic expression of his individuality and his ability to understand and appreciate a sophisticated art form. In this way, it could form another part of a positive and sympathetic understanding of the character of Alex in the novel.

The relationship between the book and the film is discussed by Morrison when he considers the crucial significance of the last chapter. He defends it against criticisms by Kubrick and the American publisher who wanted it removed on the grounds of it being too optimistic and bland. Morrison points out that Alex has always been presented in the novel as someone who learns from others (see the 'Commentary' for Part 1, Chapter 2), and in the course of time he is able to learn from Pete that there is more to life than violence and drugs. As he also points out, the novel does not end on a note of triumphalism (see the 'Commentary' on the last chapter), and there is no wonderful happy ending.

Morrison's essay also raises the question of whether *A Clockwork Orange* is, as Burgess himself put it, 'a work too didactic to be artistic'. This is related to the earlier discussion of the book's last chapter and the charge that the ending is too simplistic and optimistic. Just as that criticism is misplaced, the charge of didacticism is also off the mark because it fails to take account of the complexity with which the theme of free will is dealt with in the novel. This can be approached by way of the book's treatment of crime and punishment. Alex's brutality is not underplayed and, even though there are likeable aspects to his character, it is not easy to forget the sheer nastiness of his criminal acts. Dr Brodsky says that he is only interested in reducing crime, and the way in which crime is presented in the early chapters makes it easy to see his point of view. Nor does the author evade the uncomfortable fact that Alex chooses to act like this. The freedom to choose can come into direct conflict with other valuable principles, like the freedom to walk down a street without being viciously attacked. By presenting both points of view, and by having Alex grow from being an adolescent into a mature young man, the author avoids a simplistic didacticism.

FURTHER RESOURCES

Anthony Burgess, *You've Had Your Time, Being the Second Part of The Confessions of Anthony Burgess* (Penguin, 1990). There is not a great deal of information about the writing of *A Clockwork Orange* but it is worth looking at a copy in a library and looking up the references to the book and the film in the index.

A Clockwork Orange, directed by Stanley Kubrick. The film of the book, minus the last chapter, is available for rental in video stores.

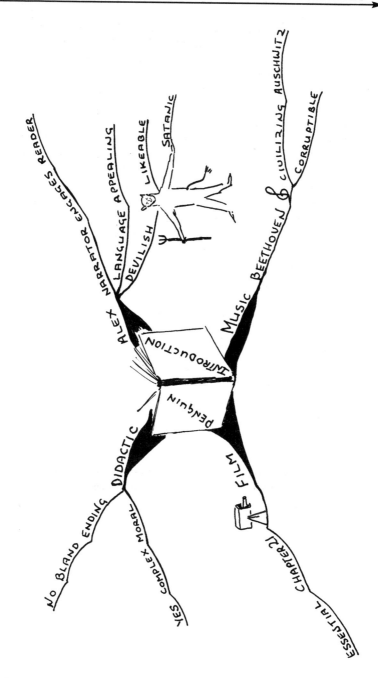

In all your study, in coursework, and in exams, be aware of the following:

- **Characterization** – the characters and how we know about them (e.g. speech, actions, author description), their relationships, and how they develop.
- **Plot and structure** – story and how it is organized into parts or episodes.
- **Setting and atmosphere** – the changing physical scene and how it reflects the story (e.g. a storm reflecting chaos).
- **Style and language** – the author's choice of words, and literary devices such as imagery, and how these reflect the **mood**.
- **Viewpoint** – how the story is told (e.g. in the first person, through a narrator, as in *A Clockwork Orange*).
- **Social and historical context** – the author's influences (see 'Context').
- **Critical approaches** – different ways in which the text has been, or could be, interpreted.

Develop your ability to:

- Relate **detail** to broader **content, meaning** and **style**.
- Show understanding of the author's **intentions, technique and meaning** (brief and appropriate comparisons with other works by the same author will gain marks).
- Give **personal response and interpretation**, backed up by **examples** and short **quotations**.
- **Evaluate** the author's achievement (how far does she/he succeed – give reasons).

Make sure you:

- Use **paragraphs** and **sentences** correctly.
- Write in an appropriate **register** – formal but not stilted.
- Use short, appropriate quotations as **evidence** of your understanding.
- Use **literary terms** correctly to explain how an author achieves effects.

THE EXAM ESSAY

Planning

You will probably have about 45 minutes for one essay. It is worth spending 5–10 minutes planning it. An excellent way to do this is in the three stages below.

1 **Mind Map** your ideas, without worrying about their order yet.
2 **Order** the relevant ideas (the ones that really relate to the question) by numbering them in the order in which you will write the essay.
3 **Gather** your evidence and short quotations.

You could remember this as the **MOG** technique.

Writing and checking

Then write the essay, allowing five minutes at the end for checking relevance, spelling, grammar and punctuation.

Remember!

Stick to the question and always **back up** your points with evidence in the form of examples and short quotations. Note: you can use '…' for unimportant words missed out in a quotation.

Model answer and plan

The next (and final) chapter consists of an answer to an exam question on *A Clockwork Orange*, with the Mind Map and plan used to write it. Don't be put off if you think you couldn't write an essay like this yet. You'll develop your skills if you work at them. Even if you're reading this the night before the exam, you can easily memorize the MOG technique in order to do your personal best.

The model answer and plan are good examples to follow, but don't learn them by heart. It's better to pay close attention to the wording of the question you choose to answer, and allow Mind Mapping to help you think creatively and structurally. Before reading the answer, you might like to do a plan of your own to compare with the example. The numbered points, with comments at the end, show why it's a good answer.

M ODEL ANSWER AND AND ESSAY PLAN

QUESTION

How important is the concept of free will in *A Clockwork Orange*?

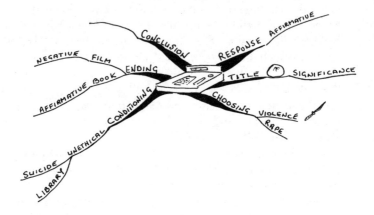

PLAN

- General response to the question, asserting the central importance of free will.
- Consider the title's significance.
- Show how free will can lead to choosing sexual violence.
- Show how conditioning reduces Alex to the state of a clockwork toy.
- Importance of the ending in terms of the essay title.
- Conclusion, reaffirming what was said in the first paragraph.

ESSAY

The question of free will, and the role it plays in being human, is the central theme of *A Clockwork Orange*. Free will is the freedom to make a choice and, even if what is chosen is bad, the principle of free will is not something to be compromised. The idea that exercising free will is essential to being a person underlies the novel's philosophical nature.[1]

The centrality of this theme is reflected in the novel's title. In Chapter 2, when Alex reads from the manuscript in the cottage that he has broken into, he discovers that the man is writing a book called *A Clockwork Orange*. The writer of the manuscript argues that a person is a living, developing being, a 'creature of growth and capable of sweetness, like an orange'. An attempt to control and direct the behaviour of such a being is ethically wrong because it reduces a person to the level of a machine. Hence the image of a clockwork orange. We find out later that the writer of the manuscript has a political agenda of his own in the novel's plot, but the point he is making here remains valid. Burgess does not merely assert its value, for such a didactic approach would reduce the novel's claim to be a work of art. Instead, he uses Alex's experiences to show the consequences of treating a person like a machine. The theme that gives depth and meaning to the image of a clockwork orange, an image of a human being controlled like a mechanism, is that of free will.[2]

Alex feels intuitively the importance of free will when he observes a drugged customer in the milkbar in the first chapter. Alex takes certain drugs as a stimulant, and he shows contempt for the customer who loses his identity under the influence of other drugs. 'You lost your name and your body and your self and you just didn't care,' he says. Alex, on the other hand, is very aware of himself and what he wants, and in the following chapter we see him freely choosing to beat and rape. It is significant that the image of a person as a growing, developing being, the image of a clockwork orange, occurs in a situation which is particularly nasty and brutal. The author wants to draw attention to the uncomfortable idea that free will may involve the kind of choices made by Alex and his gang. This idea is emphasized again in Chapter 4 when Alex shows an awareness of his ethical nature and the fact that he is choosing to act in the way he does because he enjoys it. Acting in a bad or a good way is a matter of choice, he reasons, and so 'badness is of the self, the one, the you or me'. Just as some people choose to be good, he reasons, he happens to choose to be bad. The chapter ends with a defiant demonstration of this when he exploits two gullible young girls by luring them back to his room.[3]

The challenge to the value of free will comes in the form of Ludovico's Technique, a form of conditioning that brainwashes the mind to associate violence with physical discomfort and pain. Alex is 'cured' in the sense that whenever he even thinks of something violent his body reacts with such distress that he is forced to think and act in a contrary way. Part 2 ends with a graphic proof of this when we see Alex down on his knees trying to lick the boots of the person who beats him. Alex has become a clockwork orange, programmed to avoid violence. He has lost his free will because his submissive behaviour is a conditioned response brought about by the Pavlovian method of treatment to which he has been subjected.[4]

The prison chaplain voices his ethical objection to the treatment by stressing the primacy of free will. Even though a person may choose to act criminally, it is a moral crime to remove the freedom to make that choice. The chaplain asks whether a man who chooses to be bad is 'perhaps in some way better' than someone who is forced against his will to be good. This way of thinking lies at the philosophical heart of the novel. To exercise one's free will is part of being human. It is what allows us to speak in moral terms in the first place. To reduce man to a machine robs him of this essential part of his nature. This is why the chaplain can say, 'It may not be nice to be good, little 6655321. It may be horrible to be good.'[5] Being good is only meaningful when the person has the option of behaving badly; if there is no choice then acting in a good way loses its value.

Alex cries out that he has been sinned against when he hears the music of Beethoven as a soundtrack for the violent images he is being conditioned to reject. Burgess presents the denial of free will in theological terms, as an ethical crime against humanity. Dr Brodsky and the government minister do not see it in this way, because they are only interested in reducing the crime rate and the prison population. The reader is persuaded that the chaplain has a point when, in the library scene, Alex himself is attacked. There is something laughable about Alex's plight, and one can sympathize with the anger of the elderly citizens. However, Alex's situation is humiliating. His lack of control over his own behaviour makes him incapable of dealing with certain situations. In his dealings with F. Alexander and his associates, this is taken to an extreme and we see Alex being driven to attempt suicide.[6]

The importance of free will in the novel may be appreciated in the light of the film version, which follows early American editions of the book that omitted the last chapter. Alex returns to his normal state and promptly resumes his old way of life. 'I was cured all right,' the ironic last words of the penultimate chapter proclaim. The film version ends on this note as it shows Alex indulging once again in sex and violence. When Burgess first saw the film, he was concerned. As he later stated: 'A vindication of free will had become an exaltation of the urge to sin. I was worried.'[7] The novel has shown Alex exercising his free will in thoroughly unpleasant ways. Nevertheless, the author does not want to revel in this and proclaim it in the way the film's ending manages to do. Instead, as the last chapter shows, Alex is also capable of growing up and maturing. The book ends with Alex exercising his free will and choosing to change his way of life. This ending vindicates what the chaplain and F. Alexander were saying and stresses the vital importance of the idea of free will in *A Clockwork Orange*.[8]

WHAT EARNED THE MARKS?

1 Concise introduction, focusing on the question and the writer's response. A brief summary of the assertion that the essay will go on to develop.
2 Elaboration of the significance of the novel's title and the way it relates to the theme of free will. This keeps the essay question firmly in focus.
3 An example involving Alex's exercise of free will, showing the negative aspects of being free to make choices.
4 Shows how Ludovico's Technique removes his free will. The reference to Pavlov shows an awareness of the novel's social context.
5 Appropriate use of a short quotation.
6 Examples to support the chaplain's point of view.
7 Shows knowledge of the author's attitude, using a suitable quotation.
8 Uses the last chapter to conclude and return to the essay title.

It is important to realize that the above essay does not represent the only way of successfully dealing with the essay title. It is also worth remembering that, at nearly 1200 words, this essay is probably longer than what you will have time to write under examination conditions.

It would be difficult to answer this essay question by arguing that free will is not important in the novel, but that does not mean that the essay above is the only way to tackle the question. Other episodes in the text could be introduced and discussed. For example, in discussing Alex's attitude towards certain drugs it would be possible to refer to the scene in Part 3 where he returns to the milkbar and this time takes the kind of *cowardly* drug he had previously rejected. In losing his free will, Alex loses the will to live and take control of his life and this emerges in his hallucinogenic daydream, in which he experiences a terrible sense of loss and emptiness.

Examiners will give the highest marks to a clearly structured essay. This is why it is worth drawing a quick Mini Mind Map in response to the essay title in order to organize your thoughts. It is also important that you remain focused on the question and that all your examples serve to illustrate points that are relevant to the essay title. For example, in the essay above, it would not be useful to discuss Alex's violence in terms of the state violence used against him or to look at the way violence is accepted in his society. Such issues would be relevant to an essay about the treatment of violence in the novel, but not free will. In the essay above, Alex's violence is best discussed in terms of his free will.

GLOSSARY OF LITERARY TERMS

aesthetic   concerned with appropriate taste, sensitive to good taste.

alliteration   the repetition, for effect, of consonant sounds.

allusion   the use of literary, cultural and historical references.

assonance   the repetition, for effect, of vowel sounds.

caricature   exaggeration and simplification of character traits.

characterization   the way characters are presented, not the characters themselves.

context   the background of social, historical and literary influences on a work.

dialect   regional form of language varying from the standard in vocabulary and grammar.

diction   choice and arrangement of words.

didactic   intended to instruct; in literary criticism, often used in negative sense.

discursive   presenting a logical argument, step by step.

epistolary novel   genre of fiction in which the plot unfolds through letters.

feminist criticism   critical approach developed in the 1960s, based on assessing the role of gender in texts. A particular issue is the subordination of women in a patriarchal society.

free indirect speech   technique of blending a character's words and thoughts with those of the narrator.

genre   type of literary work conforming to certain expectations; e.g. tragedy.

Gothic novel   genre of fiction popular in the eighteenth century, in which eerie and supernatural events take place in sinister settings.

idiom   a characteristic expression of a language or **dialect**.

image   a word picture bringing an idea to life by appealing to the senses; a clockwork orange is the central image in the book that carries the name as its title.

industrial novel   novel dealing with the issues of the Industrial Revolution, often set in the north of England; e.g. *North and South* by Elizabeth Gaskell.

irony   a style of writing in which one thing is said and another is meant, used for a variety of effects, such as criticism or ridicule.

magical realism   a fiction style which combines mythical elements, bizarre events and a strong sense of cultural tradition; e.g. *Midnight's Children* by Salman Rushdie.

Marxist criticism   critical approach which sees literature in relation to class struggle, and assesses the way texts present social realities.

melodrama   sensational dramatic piece appealing to the emotions, usually ending happily.

metaphor   a compressed **simile** describing something as if it were something else.

narrator   in a novel, a character who tells the story. An *omniscient* narrator has complete knowledge of everything that takes place in the narrative; an *unreliable* narrator is one whose knowledge and judgements are limited and biased.

nasdat   Russian word for teenage; the name of the language spoken by Alex and his gang.

onomatopoeia   use of words whose sound imitates the thing they describe.

paradox   an apparently contradictory statement which contains some truth; e.g. 'I hear her hair has turned quite gold from grief' (*The Importance of Being Earnest*).

parody   an exaggerated copy (especially of a writer's style) made for humorous effect.

persona   an assumed identity.

personification   an **image** speaking of something abstract, such as love, death or sleep, as if it were a person or a god.

picaresque   type of novel popular in the eighteenth century, featuring the adventures of a wandering rogue; e.g. *Tom Jones* by Henry Fielding.

plot   the story; the events that take place and how they are arranged.

polemical   (of style) making an argument.

rhetorical   expressed with a view to persuade (often used in negative sense).

satire   literature which humorously exposes and ridicules vice and folly.

simile   an **image** comparing two things similar in some way but different in others, normally using 'like' or 'as'.

standard English   the particular form of English, originally based on East Midlands dialect, most often used by educated speakers in formal situations.

stream of consciousness   technique exploring the thought processes and unconscious minds of characters; used by writers such as Virginia Woolf and James Joyce.

structure   the organization of a text; e.g. narrative, plot, repeated images and symbols.

subplot   subsidiary plot coinciding with the main plot and often reflecting aspects of it.

tone   the mood created by a writer's choice and organization of words; e.g. persuasive.

viewpoint   the way a narrator approaches the material and the audience.

INDEX

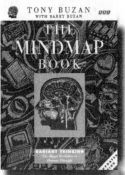